Splendid International Praise for *An Exclusive Love*

"The most impressive opening sentence of this literary season."
—*Libération*, France

"Exclusive, that is to say *singular*, in every way: in its project, in its realization, and in its translation. A breathtaking fairy tale of suicide."
—Irène Heidelberger-Leonard, Free University of Brussels, Belgium

"A story that is troubling in its immediacy, and which, via an intuitive sensitivity, captures a striking truth. . . . Very simply, without pathos, without artifice, this personal account is written with the infinite gentleness of sorrow that has found peace."
—*Le Monde*, France

"A remarkable book. . . . [It] succeeds so profoundly— the sequences flow through time and space and from one person's voice to another with calm assurance, like a great musical composition."
—*Sunday Star Times*, New Zealand

"Her simple and direct style renders the story with a perfect clarity."
—*Le Figaro*, France

"A beautiful book."
—*L'Express,* France

"The fact that the author does not tire in inquiring into this riddle, that she scrutinizes everything anew, courageously and with a biting wit, makes her book about a grim Sunday a sparkling work." —*Frankfurter Allgemeine Zeitung*, Germany

"*An Exclusive Love* is a wonderful narrative about an extraordinary couple—enchanting, warm, and consoling."
—*Buch Journal*, Germany

"A stirring account of sorrow and heartbreak."
—*Vogue*, Australia

"Best described as literary nonfiction, this memoir moved me to laughter and tears." —*Herald Sun*, Australia

"Adorján has written a book that shimmers with a sense of the casual comedy of human life. . . . It is certainly the work of a natural writer, graceful as well as forceful. . . . *An Exclusive Love* is one of the most striking memoirs to be published anywhere in years." —*The Australian*, Australia

"This is an intense, complex, uplifting, passionate, painful, and often hilarious story of love."
—Lily Brett, author of *Things Could be Worse*

"A very poignant book." —*Die ZEIT*, Germany

An Exclusive Love

Johanna Adorján

Translated by Anthea Bell

W. W. Norton & Company New York   London

Eine exklusive Liebe
by Johanna Adorján
Copyright © 2009 by Luchterhand Literaturverlag, a division of Verlagsgruppe, Random House
GmbH, Munich, Germany.

English translation copyright © Anthea Bell, 2010

First published in German in 2009 by Luchterhand Literaturverlag, a division of Verlagsgruppe,
Random House GmbH, Munich, Germany.

First published in English in 2010 by The Text Publishing Company, Australia.

First American Edition 2011

For information about permission to reproduce selections from this book, write to Permissions,
W. W. Norton & Company, Inc., 500 Fifth Avenue, New York, NY 10110

For information about special discounts for bulk purchases, please contact W. W. Norton Special
Sales at specialsales@wwnorton.com or 800-233-4830

Manufacturing by Courier Westford
Production manager: Anna Oler

Library of Congress Cataloging-in-Publication Data

Adorján, Johanna, 1971–
    [Exklusive Liebe. English]
    An exclusive love / Johanna Adorján ; translated by Anthea Bell. — 1st American ed.
        p. cm.
    "First published in German in 2009 by Luchterhand Literaturverlag . . . Munich,
Germany"—T.p. verso.
    "First published in English in 2010 by the Text Publishing Company, Australia"—T.p. verso.
    ISBN 978-0-393-08001-8 (hardcover)
1. Adorján, Johanna, 1971– —Family. 2. Jews—Hungary—Biography. 3. Jews,
Hungarian—Denmark—Biography. 4. Holocaust survivors—Denmark—Charlottenlund—
Biography. 5. Grandparents—Denmark—Charlottenlund—Biography. 6. Grandparents—
Death—Case studies. 7. Suicide pacts—Case studies. 8. Charlottenlund (Denmark)—
Biography. 9. Adorján, Johanna, 1971– 10. Grandchildren of Holocaust survivors—
Biography. I. Title.
    DS135.H93A11 2011
    940.53'180922—dc22

                                    2010035381

W. W. Norton & Company, Inc.
500 Fifth Avenue, New York, N.Y. 10110
www.wwnorton.com

W. W. Norton & Company Ltd.
Castle House, 75/76 Wells Street, London W1T 3QT

1 2 3 4 5 6 7 8 9 0

For my father

On 13 October 1991 my grandparents killed themselves. It was a Sunday. Not really the ideal day of the week for suicide. On Sundays family members call each other, friends drop in to go walking their dogs with you. I'd have thought a Monday, for instance, much more suitable. But there we are, it was a Sunday, it was in October. I picture a clear autumn day, because it all happened in Denmark. My grandparents lived in Charlottenlund, a suburb of Copenhagen where all the houses have gardens and you call your neighbours by their first names. I imagine that my grandmother was the first to wake that morning; I imagine her waking up, and her first thought is that this is the last morning she will ever wake up. She will never wake up again, and she will only go to sleep once more. My grandmother sits up quickly, pushes back the covers and puts on the slippers that she leaves neatly beside the bed every evening. Then she gets to her feet, a slender woman of seventy-one, smooths out her nightdress, and quietly, so as not to wake my grandfather, she walks the few metres to the door.

In the corridor she is welcomed by Mitzi the dog, wagging her tail. Mitzi is an Irish terrier bitch, a nice dog, phlegmatic, not particularly obedient. My grandmother gets on well with her. She speaks Hungarian to Mitzi. 'Jó kis kutya,' says my grandmother when she has quietly closed the bedroom door, good little dog. She has a low bass voice like a man's, probably as a result of all those cigarettes, she's a chain-smoker. In my imagined picture of that morning, I could go back again and place a lighted cigarette between her fingers directly after she wakes up, Prince Denmark brand, extra strong (advertising slogan: Prince Denmark for Real Men). Yes, she'll have lit herself a cigarette once she had her slippers on, at the latest. So as she pats the dog's head in the passage, quietly closing the bedroom door behind her, the air smells of fresh smoke.

A little later the smell of coffee mingles with the cigarette smoke. A keen nose would also pick up a hint of Jicky by Guerlain. My grandmother has her dressing-gown on, a silk kimono that my father once brought her back from Japan; she wears it loosely belted around her waist, and now she is sitting at the kitchen table. She holds a lighted cigarette between the fingers of her left hand. She has long, elegant fingers, and holds the cigarette very close to her fingertips, as if a cigarette were something precious. My grandmother is waiting for the coffee to finish filtering through the machine. A fountain pen and a pad of paper lie on the table in front of her.

Anyone seeing my grandmother now might think she was bored. Her eyebrows arch so far above her eyes that they always look as if she were raising them. Heavy lids lend her features a slightly blasé weariness. In photographs from her young days my grandmother looks a little like Liz Taylor. Or Lana Turner. Or some other film star of that period with long dark hair and chiselled cheekbones. She has a short, straight nose and a small mouth with a curving lower lip. Her eyelashes are perhaps a little too short to be perfect, and they are dead straight.

Even on this day, the last day of her life, she is still a beautiful woman. Her skin is tanned a deep, almost dirty brown by the summer sun. Her cheekbones seem to have risen even higher. She wears her hair in a chin-length bob. With the years it has become wiry, and surrounds her face like a thick, dark grey hood. On the morning of 13 October 1991 my grandmother sits at the kitchen table. As she waits for the coffee to run through the machine, she makes notes of things to do on her spiral-bound pad. Cancel the newspaper, she writes. Get the roses ready for winter. She isn't wearing glasses, she doesn't need them even at the age of seventy-one, and she is very proud of the fact. A cigarette glows in the ashtray on the table in front of her. It crackles faintly as the glow eats its way further into the paper. My grandmother writes: Mitzi. When she puts the pen down, a little ink drops off the nib, spreads into a blue mark on the paper and makes the word Mitzi invisible. Never mind. She's not going to forget about Mitzi. Over the last few days she has gone over her list so often that she can recite the items on it by heart anyway. She switches on the radio, a small, portable plastic set standing beside the toaster. The music is something by Bach. It's Sunday, after all.

‡

On the morning of 13 October 1991, my grandfather emerges from sleep with a stertorous breath, and is instantly wide awake. He reaches for his glasses, which are lying on the bedside table, and glances at the alarm clock. Nine a.m. He knows what day this is. He doesn't have to remember what it's about, he knew even in his sleep. Sounds come from the kitchen, the sounds you hear when someone is trying to empty the dishwasher particularly quietly. Also quietly playing is Bach's A minor violin concerto. Is it the Menuhin recording? He lies there for another few bars, then sits up, which is an effort. Every movement tires him, and once sitting he has to rest for a moment. Then, as if giving himself a little shake, he smooths his hair back and down at the sides, where it ought to be. Very slowly, he stands up.

People who visited my grandparents in the last weeks of their lives, who entered their cavernous little house, smoke-filled and cosy, crammed with objects, either did not see my grandfather at all, because he was asleep, or they found him on the living-room sofa, tired and very thin. In the space of a few months his weight had dropped from 70 to 58 kilos, and he looked as if he had shrunk. He sat propped on cushions, and did not rise to his feet even when visitors left. He had heart trouble. His heart muscle was weakened, a phenomenon of old age, or perhaps the long-term result of a typhoid infection he had suffered during the wars. The doctors gave him only a few months to live, and by the end he had an oxygen inhaler by his bed to which he could resort for air.

I knew him only when his hair was white. A man of distinguished appearance, a side parting in his hair, a moustache, a strong, dimpled chin. He always wore good shirts, often with a silk cravat around his neck, and his eyebrows were long and bushy and stood out in so many directions that they seemed to lead a life of their own. I have a photograph of him in a doctor's coat and surgical mask, eyebrows bristling above the rims of his glasses—you can recognise him at once. He was an orthopaedic surgeon, specialising in disorders of the legs and feet. When I was a child he diagnosed my flat feet, but he told me so nicely that I thought it was a compliment.

To other people he may have looked like a perfectly ordinary white-haired elderly gentleman with bushy eyebrows. And my grandmother may have looked to others like a perfectly normal elderly lady whose posture, if you stopped to notice the details, was remarkably upright. Their effect on me was something like this:

Enter my grandparents from Copenhagen. An elegant couple looking as if they had just parked their vintage car round the corner. They step out of a cloud of perfume and cigarette smoke. They have the deepest voices ever heard, they speak German with a foreign accent, and they talk to me as if I were a grown-up but on a small scale. Do you like ballet, are you interested in opera, do you think extraterrestrial life is possible? Not in her wildest dreams would my grandmother have considered crawling round the playroom with her grandchildren, searching for a cap lost from a Playmobil character that just had to be somewhere. Instead, she went to the opera with us. And when I was five years old my grandfather let me puff his cigar—I had a terrible coughing fit and he was horrified, and quickly bought me an ice-cream. They seemed to me like film stars, attractive and mysterious, and the fact that they were related to me, were my own forebears, made them absolutely irresistible.

‡

Cut to a peaceful Austrian landscape near Linz. Gently rolling green hills. And on top of one of the hills, like a toy castle, lies the former concentration camp of Mauthausen, now a museum. It looks harmless, like a miniature model of something much larger. As if the scale had slipped—it's so easy to see the full extent of the place. Two little towers with battlements and a heavy wooden gate. If there were a river in front of it you could imagine a drawbridge here, but there's only a footpath winding its way up the hill to outside the gate, which is wider than it is high. A small door is fitted into the right-hand side of the gate, and stands open. Anyone can go through it—it works both ways, in and out. Sometimes, when there are too many visitors, you get temporary traffic jams, but everyone who goes in will come out again. Once through the door you go a little way down the slope, past signs saying 'The Stairs of Death', all splendidly converted for the museum. You go a few steps down, past the main entrance to the parking place where lots of buses wait from midday onwards, you pay your parking ticket, so easy these days with the euro, and you drive home, relieved, moved, exhausted, and where's the bottle of water, and can we please stop at a service station with a toilet, and how much longer will this toll sticker be valid?

I'm here with my father. On the night before our visit I dreamed that there were visitors' books lying around the concentration camp, listing the former prisoners. In my dream I leafed through them, and suddenly I recognised my grandfather's writing among the entries. 'Mit kap a kutya. Kakilni, pisilni,' it said in Hungarian. 'What does the dog get? Shit, piss.' And then his signature.

It is early in the morning, we are almost the first visitors. My father and I stand for a while on the former parade ground, 350 metres long where it stretches out before us in the sunlight. A beautiful day. Hot. Not a cloud in the sky. Now and then a fly buzzes through the air. There's something about it that suggests a holiday camp, the place is so peaceful, the birds twittering, the sun shining. We don't know exactly what we're supposed to do, so first we go to watch a documentary film shown every hour, on the hour, in one of the huts around the parade ground. The screening is in a room that reminds me of a classroom. Rows of old cinema seats for the audience, the wooden seats squeal as you fold them down and soon turn out to be uncomfortable. The film is projected on the front wall of the room; it is rather an old print, with a crackle on the soundtrack and not much contrast in the picture, so that now and then there's a good deal that you can't make out.

The film shows a stone quarry. Hundreds of men in striped prison clothing drag heavy blocks of granite up a steep flight of steps. These, explains the commentator, are the Stairs of Death, as they were known, and countless people died on those steps, some from exhaustion, some from ill-treatment by the SS guards. Mauthausen was a Category III camp. Category III meant 'extermination through labour'. The screen now shows an almost vertical rock wall about 50 metres high, called by the SS the 'parachute-jump wall'. SS men flung prisoners to their death from the top of it; a thousand died on the day when Himmler visited the camp in March 1943.

Pictures of dead bodies caught on electric fences, eye-witnesses speaking of what they saw. 'You wouldn't believe it if you hadn't seen it with your own eyes,' says one man, in a heavy Austrian accent. 'A lot of people think it's not true, but no one really believes that.' Then comes the story of the five hundred Russian prisoners who managed to escape in January 1945. Eleven of them survived the hunt for them by SS men and local residents. Eleven out of five hundred. On 5 May Mauthausen was liberated by the Americans. The US soldier who is telling the story in the film, now an old man, keeps breaking down as his tears flow.

The film shot on the day of liberation shows men reduced to skeletons, in striped prison clothing with the Star of David on their chests. All their heads are shaven, they have huge eyes and noses, mouths that are mere lines in their faces, and long, thin fingers; the only difference between them is in their height. Out of the corner of my eye I see my father putting a finger under his glasses a couple of times during the film. I don't dare to turn and look at him. Neither of us says much after the film is over, and when we do our voices are deliberately casual. I didn't know there was a gas chamber in Mauthausen, I say. No, says my father, nor did he.

After that we go on a guided tour through the camp. Our guide is a young man in trainers, shorts and a polo shirt. The parade ground where we're standing is reflected in the metallic silver lenses of his sunglasses. It is covered with gravel, and the heavy roller that the prisoners were forced to use to keep it smooth still stands here. By now we are surrounded by schoolchildren. They make a lot of noise, they laugh, they send text messages. Do they know why they're here? Does it interest them? Is it enough that they're here at all? I feel anger rising in me; I am angry with these ugly teenagers, their hair dyed too black, their jeans too low-slung.

Our guide recites the facts in his Austrian accent. 'The hut over there, look, please, that's where they removed vital organs from the prisoners, live prisoners, to see how long they would survive. Most of them died in agony. So if you would please now look to your right.' His bored tone of voice deprives the horrors of their full force. Is that good, is that bad? I don't know. I am glad I'm not in too much danger of weeping. I'd been afraid of that. Of finding myself shedding tears here in front of my father. But here I am, standing around in the heat, thinking I ought to have brought sun screen with a higher SPF factor, wondering whether to buy a Diet Coke on the way out, and at the same time hearing about the horror that is still so present to my mind, although I couldn't have given it a precise name. Standing here, my overriding thought is: but my grandfather survived it. He did survive it.

A museum in the basement contains records of medical experiments. 'In this hut perfectly healthy people had their organs removed, and observations were made of the time they could live without, for instance, their kidneys,' recites our guide. 'They very soon died in terrible pain. Now, if you would please follow me.' A few metres further on he tells us how tattooed prisoners had their skin removed and made into lampshades, as we know from Auschwitz. There's a picture in a display case behind him. The group gathers in front of it, the indistinct black and white photograph of a lampshade with little anchors on it. I move away from the group a couple of times to look more closely at the photographs in the glass cases. I am always prepared—even eager—to recognise my grandfather as one of those thin figures. What was it like for him in Mauthausen? He would never talk about that time. Did he work in the stone quarry? Or as a doctor? What did Jewish doctors do in a concentration camp? Which patients could they have treated for what?

We go through a room dedicated to the memory of the victims—photos of prisoners are displayed here with their names and dates of birth and death, though most of them are Italians, and again my grandfather is not there—and then comes the gas chamber. It is not especially large, and has a low ceiling. I just want to get out of this place. I already hear the voices of the next group following close behind us. Girlish giggling makes its way into the gas chamber. I feel emotions suddenly rising in me, I don't know quite what they are, anger, grief? Somehow it is all a bit too much at the moment, and I would like to be alone. On the way out we go through a small room with a gallows in it. However, most of the people killed in this room were shot at the base of the neck, our guide tells us, it was more practical, 'if only for reasons of speed'. Then he delivers a brief lecture on the present neo-Nazi situation in Austria, telling us that swastika graffiti have to be removed almost daily from the walls of the gas chamber. He says how much that distresses him, but he says it in the same indifferent voice that he has used for the rest of his programme. 'And now we have come to the end of our tour. Thank you very much, and if you have any more questions…'

‡

My grandfather has put a dressing-gown on over his pyjamas, and he is wearing gentlemen's dark leather slippers when he comes into the kitchen. He is dragging himself along rather than walking. The radio is still on, now playing Bach's double concerto for two violins.

'Good morning.' His voice is even deeper than my grandmother's, a growling bass.

'Good morning,' says my grandmother. 'Did you sleep well?' All their lives they used the formal, polite form of the pronoun 'you', something most unusual even among Hungarians of their generation—and Hungarians married to each other at that.

'No, not very well,' says my grandfather. 'What about you?'

My grandmother's face wears a dismissive expression.

My grandfather sits down. 'Haven't you brought the newspaper in yet?'

'It's Sunday,' says my grandmother,

'Ah, so it is,' says my grandfather, as if only just remembering that himself.

My grandmother is a little edgy, although she does not

13

like to admit it even to herself. Mitzi the dog sits at her feet looking up at her devotedly. Mitzi is probably wondering whether she may get something to eat, which could indeed happen at any moment, because my grandmother does not agree with authoritarian dog-training. Or perhaps Mitzi's doggy head is completely empty. She is not a very clever dog, and if she were she would hide it. So she sits at my grand-mother's feet, looking up at her all the time, and then my grandmother does briefly pat her head, pulling at the short, wiry curls between her ears, just the way Mitzi likes it.

'When are you going to Inga's?' asks my grandfather.

'I'm supposed to be there around midday,' says my grandmother.

The radio crackles. My grandfather readjusts the aerial, moving it to the left and to the right, and finally standing it diagonally opposite the window. Then he picks up the coffee jug and pours himself a cup. He spills half of it.

My grandmother sighs.

'Oh dear,' he says, noticing his clumsiness. This kind of thing has been happening more often recently. He has diffi-culty in estimating distances properly. He assumes that's a side effect of his medication.

My grandmother stands up and tears a piece of kitchen paper off the roll hanging over the kitchen counter. She uses it to mop up the puddle of coffee. The paper soon turns brown. She crumples it up, wipes the table with it once more, and throws it in the rubbish bin. Then she sits down again and pours him a full cup.

'Thank you.'

He sips his coffee. On the radio, they are just coming to his favourite passage of the concerto. The first violinist has a warm, melting tone, it could be Oistrakh, thinks my grandfather, but he wouldn't bet on it.

'Did they say who the soloists are?' he asks.

'I wasn't paying attention,' says my grandmother, lighting a cigarette.

They listen to the music in silence for a while.

'I'll come with you, if you don't mind,' says my grandfather, after the last bar of the second movement has died away.

'I won't be gone more than ten minutes,' she says.

'I'll wait in the car.'

'Do be sensible. You haven't been out of doors for days.'

My grandfather does not reply.

'It will tire you too much,' says my grandmother.

My grandfather still does not reply.

For a while neither of them says anything.

'Oh, very well,' says my grandmother finally, breaking the silence. 'If you absolutely insist.' She pulls the dog's ears. 'But it will leave you very tired.' The dog, who doesn't like having her ears pulled, wriggles away from my grandmother's hands and retreats backwards under the table. My grandmother stands up. She puts her cup in the sink. 'But you must put on something warm.' With these words she leaves the kitchen.

My grandfather stays sitting there for a while, listening to the music. After the last note of the third movement there is a burst of applause on the radio. Will they say who the performers were now? Recently he has sometimes waited for that information in vain, they're getting more and more inclined just to announce the next piece.

He takes a flat silver case out of the pocket of his dressing-gown, opens it and takes out a cigarillo. He gets a lighter out of the other pocket, one of the kind that, it is claimed, will work even in a stormy wind. He lights the cigarillo, his first of the day and perhaps the one he enjoys most. He draws on it powerfully a couple of times, and smoke rises. Ah, listen, the applause is dying down. 'Det var dobbetconcerten af Johann Sebastian Bach, spillet af David Oistrakh og Yehudi Menuhin,' says the radio presenter in Danish. 'Nu kommer et stykke af György Ligeti.' 'György,' says my grandfather, correcting the presenter; he speaks it as a single syllable, with a soft *dy* sound at the beginning and end of the name. 'Ligeti György.' Drawing deeply on his cigarillo again, he shakes his head; would the Danes never learn?

‡

We don't know much about the time my grandfather spent in the concentration camp. Indeed, we know nothing. He never talked about it, and if you asked him, as every member of the family had about once, he replied, 'We don't talk about that.' If you asked my grandmother she said the same. 'We don't talk about that.' So how did we know he'd had to learn to sleep on his feet? If he had fallen over, or if he'd sat down, he would have been shot. That one fact we did know. That is to say, my aunt and I knew it. Whatever 'knowing' means, because my father, for instance, doesn't remember ever having heard the story. Who told it to whom? When? Is it really true? There were times when I felt exhausted out jogging, and motivated myself by thinking that I was the granddaughter of a man who could sleep on his feet. Because he had to. Because his life depended on it. And it always worked. Yes, I know, how banal.

My father calls to me. Among my grandfather's papers, which he has in a drawer somewhere, he has found a sworn statement certifying that my grandfather went to Mauthausen in the year 1944, but in 1945 was liberated from the camp at Gunskirchen, 55 kilometres from Mauthausen. That surprises us. We had thought he was liberated from Mauthausen. On the internet I find accounts of the 'death marches' when prisoners were transferred to Gunskirchen in the last weeks of the war because of overcrowding at Mauthausen. I read

17

how anyone who stopped marching, who collapsed from exhaustion, or simply bent to tie a shoelace was shot on the spot by the SS men. Children, women, men, they drew no distinctions. Those who couldn't keep up with the pace were shot. Thousands died on these marches. I am shaken when I read these things, of course I am, but also relieved. So it's true, and I am the granddaughter of this man.

‡

They were introduced to each other in Budapest in 1940, at a musical recital in a private home. In Hungary the war seemed far away, all was still peaceful there. Opinions differ on whether this private recital was at a party given by mutual friends or the apartment where my grandmother's parents lived. Anyway, the milieu was that of Jewish bourgeoisie of Budapest, and I know that the music was a piano recital and the pianist's name was István Antal (of course the Hungarians would put the names the other way around: Antal István). But I still picture a violinist, a young man with a face like Kafka's, and in my imagination the musicians play Kreisler's 'Liebesleid', so redolent of old Vienna and the mellifluous melancholy of days long gone. I imagine my grandfather sitting in one of the front rows at this recital, upright and looking ahead of him, so that the first my grandmother saw of him was the back of his head. He apparently had dark brown hair at the time. He would certainly have been sitting very upright, he always did. Perhaps he was wearing a dinner jacket; he was that kind of man.

Someone or other will have whispered to my grandmother that the young man there at the front was a surgeon, and maybe it was only then that she noticed the good-looking man, or rather the good-looking back of his head, sitting so erect as he listened to the music. There will have been an interval in which they were all glad to be able to walk around, have a drink, talk at last. All except my grandfather, probably, because he loved music more than almost anything else in the world. And then someone introduced them to each other. Veronika and István, Vera and Pista. She was twenty at the time, he was thirty-one.

Apparently my grandmother knew the first time they met that this was the man she was going to marry. Or at least, that's how she often told the story. In the family we also know what happened between them next. It's one of those stories retold so often that after a while you know it couldn't have been different, it was just like that. A family legend. The two of them made a date to go for a walk. And after that they liked each other so much that they made a date to go for another walk. And then another. Each of them thought the other was crazy about walking. They were both entirely mistaken. When that point was cleared up after a while, it's said that they were enormously relieved.

They married on 7 August 1942. A small ceremony, with their families and a few friends present. In their wedding photo she is beaming at him from one side. She has a white flower in her hair, and carries a bouquet of white calla lilies. He, a head taller than she is, looks proudly down at his beautiful bride, his brand-new wedding ring on his left hand. They had a civil wedding, neither of them believed in God. Did they promise in front of the registrar to remain faithful until death did them part, or as the Hungarians say, until the spade, the rake and the big bell parted them? Did they already know, even then, that they weren't going to wait for that?

‡

What do people do on the morning that they know will be their last? I imagine that they tidy up, get things done. Take out the rubbish, file away last month's telephone bill, fold clean underclothes and make sure to smooth out those already folded before putting them away—after all, they will be seen by the eyes of others. I imagine that two people who know that this morning is their last prefer to do things separately, so as not to be looking in each other's eyes all the time, for what is there left to be said? It will all, I assume, have been discussed before. Weeks ago, months ago. Even years ago? Perhaps they listen to music, music that is not too sad, Mozart rather than Wagner. I imagine my grandfather sitting in the living-room armchair beside the record player, smoking cigars, small, thin cigarillos, and coughing again and again, a deep bronchial cough. He is still wearing his dressing-gown, he has a box of papers on his knees, he means to look through the papers and sort them out, but he doesn't. He does not move. His eyes look into the distance at something that no one else can see. He is breathing with difficulty. Perhaps he is simply tired.

My grandmother comes into the room carrying several ashtrays. By now she has dressed, she wears a dark red corduroy shirt and a denim pinafore dress with an apron tied over it. And she is wearing sturdy shoes, because she took the dog out. She has brushed her hair, and now it stands out from her head in a way that, if you painted its shape, would be reminiscent of a fir-cone. Close on her heels the dog appears in the doorway. Mitzi hasn't left her side all morning.

'Pista?' My grandmother speaks his name in a tone of mild annoyance. Pista, the diminutive of István. There's a whispered hiss about it when she says it.

My grandfather turns his head to her. He looks surprised, he hadn't heard her coming in. Then he smiles. His wife, his beautiful wife.

'I asked you a question.'

'You did?' he says.

'Have you taken your medication?' she asks.

My grandfather briefly narrows his eyes. My grandmother interprets this as assent. She goes into the kitchen to wash the ashtrays she has collected from the guestroom and the front hall. Everything must be neat and tidy. She doesn't want to cause any hassle. No one must find her decision a nuisance.

The telephone rings.

My grandmother wipes her hands on her apron and goes back into the living room, where the phone is standing on the desk. My grandfather gets to his feet and turns the music on the radio down.

My grandmother puts the receiver to her ear.

'Yes?'

——

'God dag, Sebastian, how are you?' It's my cousin.

——

'Tomorrow? No, we can't make it tomorrow, we've already discussed that. How much longer will you be in Copenhagen?'

——

'No, tomorrow we really can't, not in the afternoon either. We have to go to the hospital tomorrow. Pista's having an examination.'

——

'Yes, quite sure. It always takes a long time. Yes, a great shame, but you must come and see us some other time.'

—

'I'll do that. Goodbye for now, yes, and the same to you, farvel, farvel.'

She puts the phone down, stands up and goes back into the kitchen.

'What did he say?' my grandfather calls after her.

'He wanted to come and see us tomorrow,' my grandmother calls back.

'What did you tell him?' calls my grandfather, who had been listening to the whole conversation.

'I said we had to go to the hospital.'

'Tomorrow?'

'I said you were having an examination.'

'Right.'

'He's in Copenhagen. He wanted to come and see us tomorrow, so I said we couldn't manage it.'

'Right.'

My grandfather turns the sound up again.

In the kitchen, my grandmother briefly props both hands on the sink for support. Then she straightens up and takes an ashtray out of the water to dry it.

No, wrong, that's just my sentimental imagination. My grandmother didn't need to support herself on anything. She had made her decision, she had come to that decision long ago, and if she had been sentimental she'd still be alive today.

On that October day sixteen years ago, she was a perfectly healthy woman of seventy-one.

‡

After her death we cleared out her wardrobe, my aunt, my mother and I. I took a jacket that looks like snakeskin but is really plastic. My grandmother made it herself. The material looks so genuine that I've had to put up with snide remarks from animal conservationists when I was wearing it. By now the plastic has worn away in a couple of places near the collar, showing the green inner lining, but I still wear it. With an odd sense of family pride. Although only on chilly days, because as it's plastic you sweat inside it, although of course my grandmother never let anyone notice that.

She dressed extravagantly. She wore the plastic snake-skin jacket with trousers of the same material, and she managed not to look as if she were in fancy dress because of her inborn elegance; she simply looked good. Everything suited her. She could wear what she liked—and she did. She had a preference for striking jewellery and bold colours, combining leather and knitted fabrics, velour and corduroy, belting her slender waist with all sorts of things, and in summer she wore ankle-length yellow terry towelling and sunglasses behind which she almost disappeared.

The only thing that didn't really seem to suit the rest of

her appearance was her shoes, which we found neatly lined up in pairs in a special cupboard. My grandmother had something the matter with her feet, presumably ganglions, which I had never seen, and nor had almost everyone else because she carefully avoided ever showing her feet. She turned them slightly inwards as she walked, and she always wore flat, sturdy shoes with old-lady pale rubber soles. Not that they ever prevented her from walking proudly upright. She made her way along pavements as if walking over a red carpet that no one else could see.

If she really couldn't stand someone, she would look straight through that person, so comprehensively that, so far as the object of her scrutiny was concerned, the temperature seemed to drop several degrees. Then she acted as if the other person did not exist, even if they were face to face. She just looked through him as if she could see the other side of the street through his head, but there was nothing to be seen there either. She was both feared and admired. When she entered a room full of people, they all took their tone from her, so strong and forceful was her personality. If she laughed, they were relieved. If she was tired or—God forbid—in a bad temper, the atmosphere in general could lapse into a mood of depression.

I don't think my grandmother was aware of the effect she had on others. I think she saw herself as an elegant, interesting, clever and likeable woman who enjoyed cooking and baking and going to the opera. But what do any of us know about our grandmothers?

‡

The little woman sitting in front of me on a Biedermeier-style sofa with curving lines, on a hot summer's day in Budapest, was her best friend. She is the age my grandmother would have been today, eighty-seven. She stoops a little, like a slightly contorted tree, but she still girlishly paints her lips a strong, bright red. This is the first time we have met. Her life took her to Charleston, South Carolina, where she has been living for many years. Now she is visiting her native Hungary for a few days, and she assumes it will be for the last time. Travelling is laborious for her.

She is dressed in the peculiar way that old people sometimes favour when the decades leave them not caring whether their own taste agrees with anyone else's. Little white Eiffel Towers dance ring-a-ring-a-roses with each other on her sleeveless black shirt, and her glasses are of such huge dimensions that they protrude from both right and left of her face. He skin lies in soft lengthwise folds on her upper arms. I recognise her ring at once: three thin, intertwined circles in different shades of gold—my grandmother's Cartier ring.

26

Once we are sitting down, Erzsi lights herself a cigarette, the first of many. She smokes Marlboros. She sits on the very edge of the sofa with her legs apart, forearms propped on her thighs, looks at me through her huge glasses. 'Okay,' she says, 'what do you want to know?'

‡

Germany occupied Hungary on 19 March 1944, not until quite late in the war. Within the next few months, in an operation organised on a vast scale never before known, they deported some 600,000 Hungarian Jews. Within two months, about 430,000 arrived in Auschwitz alone. The new Hungarian arrivals were an unusual sight in the camp. Well-nourished, because they had been spared the effects of the war for so long, healthy—and in such numbers that the murderers could hardly keep up with the job of killing them. However, the Germans were thorough. By May 1945, that is to say within a year, they had killed two-thirds of all Hungarian Jews.

When Germany occupied Hungary my grandmother had been in her third month of pregnancy. Six months later, on 26 September 1944, when the danger was at its height, she gave birth to a son, my father. We know that she hid him in a drawer for the first few months. But how did she manage to hide herself? Where was that drawer? How did she contrive to escape the ghetto and the concentration camp? We know that she had forged papers. Why did she have them and my grandfather did not? How did my grandmother survive the war?

‡

'It was a crazy time,' says Erzsi. We are speaking English to each other, I with a German and she with a Hungarian accent. Her eyes are alert behind the large lenses of her glasses. A crazy time, she says, there was so much to do, so many people to be helped. She says it with satisfaction, almost high spirits. As if it had all been a great adventure. Yet she is Jewish—how did she herself survive the German occupation?

'Forged papers,' she says in an offhand tone. 'My husband was in the Resistance, we could get hold of any amount of forged papers. It was a wonderful time—well, of course it was a terrible time, but I was in a state of elation all day long. It felt wonderful to be able to help. I was young, maybe I didn't fully understand the danger. I was chasing here and there the whole time, providing people with forged papers and feeling like a good angel.'

Yes, but if it was so simple, why did my grandfather, her best friend's husband, end up in a concentration camp?

'He was conscripted into the Jewish men's labour unit and taken away. There was nothing we could do about it. But your grandmother had forged papers. I know she wore the Jewish star for just one day, then she took it off again. But I don't know where she was living, we didn't have much contact with each other then.'

At the time, says Erzsi, my grandmother had suspected her of collaborating with the Germans. While all her acquaintances were being sent to the ghetto or disappearing she, Erszi, had been going around fearlessly, unharmed and in good spirits, and that had struck my grandmother as peculiar. And their ways had parted for a couple of years because of their husbands anyway, she adds. Both had been so much in love, not long married, there wasn't any room left in their lives for a girlfriend. But she did visit my grandmother once in hospital, Erzsi tells me, a few days before the baby came.

So my father was born in hospital?

'Yes. After all, she had her forged papers. Her mother was there too when I visited. Vera was in a shockingly bad temper.'

Erzsi laughs. Then she tells me how they met, she and my grandmother, how they had made friends at school and did everything together, homework, ballet lessons, cigarette-smoking. How they were the best of friends, because they didn't have many other friends, and I picture them to myself as prettier than the other girls in the class, prettier, more intelligent, and probably terribly arrogant.

‡

After their wedding my grandparents moved into a hand-some building near the Opera House, right on one of the busiest squares in town, the Oktogon, where four streets meet, and you can change from the tramline to the Metro. The building is still there. These days it has a neon ad mounted on its roof, with green lettering saying *Rolex* and a little yellow crown above the L, visible from afar. It's one of those southern European apartment blocks built round an inner courtyard. A stairwell links the floors as they turn their balustrades to face each other, like the tiers of seats at the theatre. Lazy people can use a lift with an iron door that opens with a rusty squeal.

My grandparents lived on the second floor. On the floor below, my grandfather's elder brother lived with his wife and child. He died in the 1960s in his new home in Australia. In photographs, he looks like a blurred watercolour sketch of my grandfather. Where my grandfather had attractively regular features, his brother's seem to have slipped, his face was thinner, his eyes rimmed with black shadows. His name was József, he was called Dodo, and he was a lawyer. We do at least know, in detail, how he survived the war. A letter exists that he wrote to a former school friend in 1946, telling him how he escaped the Gestapo more than once, and hid for the last few weeks before the end of the war in the apartment on the Oktogon, which his non-Jewish wife had been able to keep.

This is what he says about my grandparents in his letter: 'My close family members are also still alive. Pista married in 1942, and at the end of September 1944 they had a baby boy—what timing! His wife and the baby hid with forged papers through those difficult times. Pista was sent to Poland on labour service; from there they marched—making a detour around Budapest—all the way to Mauthausen and later to Gunskirchen. I assume that you are familiar with those place names through their sad claim to fame—anyway, they are in the western part of Austria.'

So we learn no more from him, either, of where my grandmother spent that time. Maybe she too was able to hide in the building on the Oktogon which, as Dodo writes, was occupied by the German Gestapo as the end of the war approached. That turned out to be lucky, because it was safe from being searched for Jews by the Hungarian Nazis who called themselves the Arrow Cross Party.

Her parents, we do know, were not so lucky. Although they too had forged papers, as Erzsi tells me, the Arrow Cross people tracked them down to their hiding-place as the end of the war drew near. It was outside Budapest, a deserted building in the country. It may have been a former factory on an island in the Danube; that's the version that my father knows. Both Erzsi and my father say that smoke rising from the chimney gave my grandmother's parents away. Like hundreds of other Jews in the last months of the war, they were driven to the banks of the Danube and shot in the river. They died in December 1944. We do not know the exact date.

My grandmother never talked about them. They lived, they were not alive now, right, so let's talk about something more cheerful.

Their names are listed on a wall at the Budapest Holocaust Memorial Centre: Gizella and Elémer Fellner. The names are very small, among those of thousands of others who were murdered. This is what my father and my aunt have told me about them: Gizella loved flowers, was a Zionist, and suffered from depression; Elémer was an engineer, he had a big moustache and a bald patch, and he was kind and amusing.

It's strange how people are remembered.

‡

The music stops at some point, although my grandfather doesn't notice, and nor does he notice my grandmother spreading the checked wool rug from the sofa over his legs. He has gone to sleep in his armchair, head on one side, mouth slightly open, and now and then his breath comes with a gurgling sound.

My grandmother has put on the yellow rubber gloves she wears for washing dishes and has rolled up her sleeves. She intends to leave the house immaculate, and after a stint of vacuuming, wiping surfaces, scrubbing and tidying the bedroom, bathroom and kitchen, it is the turn of the dining room, which is just off the living room and is seldom used. Especially since my grandfather fell ill, and they stopped asking guests to come for a meal with them.

A dark red Persian rug hangs on the wall. She is looking at it as if seeing it for the first time. It has been there ever since they moved in. Rather gloomy, really, she thinks. Funny the things that never occurred to her before. She knocks the rug with her hand, and no dust worth speaking of swirls into the air. Just as well, she thinks, otherwise she'd have had to go and search for the carpet beater.

She has let the dog out into the garden. Mitzi has probably been sitting outside the door for some time waiting to come in again, but so far my grandmother hasn't heard her barking.

There are a few envelopes on the dining table, bills: telephone, car insurance, electricity. She picks up an envelope and tries to decipher the date postmarked on the stamp. Some time in August. Without giving it another glance, she puts the whole pile in the bag of rubbish, which is already half full. She has even thought of adding her diet pills to it. And all the pairs of panties that look a little shabby. No one has to know about them.

Under the letters an ashtray comes into view. She picks it up and examines it. Seems to be clean. It is a white plastic ashtray, and on it in black lettering, decreasing in size like the letters on an optician's chart: 'Too much sex makes you short-sighted.' Pista once bought it at some airport in America. Pista, of course. That's exactly his sense of humour. He is also responsible for the clock hanging on the kitchen wall, with the words: 'No whiskey before five o'clock' inscribed on the dial. The hands stand permanently at five after five.

My grandfather's sense of humour was about as dated and full of *doubles entendres* as the cartoons in *Playboy* magazine. And just as harmless. He always told the same jokes from his small store of such things. For instance, he would say, 'My wife has legs like a gazelle,' adding roguishly, after a brief pause, 'slender and hairy.' And if anyone asked him why he and his wife used the formal 'you' pronoun to each other, he would reply, 'If I addressed my wife in familiar terms, she might get the idea of speaking to me in the same way. And that,' he would say, always shaking his head in mock horror at the very idea, 'that would never do.'

She can hear the dog outside now. Mitzi sounds as if her feelings are hurt. My grandmother puts the ashtray back on the table and straightens a chair. She looks round once again, not that there is much more to do in this room anyway. The glass-fronted cupboard with old glasses kept in the top of it and alcoholic drinks in the bottom looks freshly polished. The sheet music on the little table-piano, now so badly out of tune that Pista hardly plays it any more, is neatly stacked. 'Diabelli for four hands' lies on top. She goes quickly over to the window and adjusts the curtains where they had not been hanging straight. There, she thinks, and goes to let the dog in.

‡

I walk around Budapest, trying to imagine the city as it once was. Here and there the eastern bloc has left behind ugly brown box-shaped buildings that now accommodate hotel chains, but if you narrow your eyes and let everything blur slightly you can guess at the past. The buildings have gracefully curved entrances and inner courtyards. There are many monuments. The wind along the big boulevards beside the Danube blows your hair into your face in an annoying way. I know hardly anything about this country. The people are friendly but do not go out of their way to be civil. Men openly stare at women. Women put on weight young. The Hungarian language sounds angry.

I go through the city, trying to find out whether it touches a chord with anything in me. Whether anything here seems familiar to me, even if it's only the Hungarain mentality. When I stand on the bank of the Danube and look at the chain bridge from Pest to Buda on the other bank of the river, I think suddenly that I do remember something, in the way you remember something once heard when you were half asleep that now seems familiar, although you do not know exactly how you recognise it. Then I realise that the view simply reminds me of Prague. The Danube, the bridge, the hill on the opposite bank. Yes, just like Prague, only not quite so many bad-tempered, black-clad classes of school-children following their teachers without ever looking up from their trainer-shod feet.

Diagonally opposite the Parliament building, which is very long and so close to the banks of the Danube that the proportions look wrong, stands a monument. It is intended to remind people of the Holocaust, of the mass shootings of Jews that were carried out at this place—and at many others. As a work of art it is touchingly bad. Some twenty pairs of shoes stand on the reinforced bank, life-size and cast in metal, toes pointing to the river. They look as if someone had stolen the statues they belonged to. Or as if no one had tidied up after a barbecue. But still. Yes, it could have been here. They could have been shot here, melancholy Gizella and kindly Elémer, the Parliament building behind them, with a view of the hill of Buda, the chain bridge on the left; maybe this was the last thing they ever saw. The slope is steep here, it must be four metres down, with rocks and stones at the bottom.

When I go back to my hotel and hear the people in the streets all speaking Hungarian, I think again how much I like the language even if I don't really understand it. The sound of it, the halting rhythm that results from emphasising the first syllable of a word, the many dark vowels—it has a soothing, familiar effect on me like a childhood lullaby. I'm afraid I can communicate only with dogs in Hungarian. Hol a cica? Megyünk sétálni! Jó kutya, rossz kutya, kis kutya. Where is the cat? Let's go, good dog, bad dog. That's it. I can't even pronounce my surname properly. Once when I called my father at a Budapest hotel, the receptionist didn't understand me until I said my own Hungarian surname in broad American English. Then, finally, he put me through to Mr Adohrdshan.

How Hungarian am I really? My aunt, who has lived in Denmark since she was nine and has a Danish passport and Danish children, says she feels like a Budapest Jew. She wears a chain with two pendants on it: a cross and a Star of David. My father feels like a Dane, but by parental descent he is three-quarters Hungarian and one-quarter Croatian. My father is of Jewish origin, my mother is not. What does that make me? What does it mean to be only half all those possibilities? Is it an advantage not to have to support Germany in football matches, although I can if I like, depending on the situation? Wouldn't it be easier to be entirely something, even a one hundred per cent loser? My passport is Danish, but am I? And why do Danish passports have to be forged more frequently than those of other nationalities, so that it always takes me longer than anyone else to go through security?

‡

When I was a child I often heard people say I looked like my grandmother. I was always likely to hear it said when I was in a door-slamming mood, or simply a bad temper. It was usually my mother who said it. She was very fond of her mother-in-law, but maybe she also feared her temper a little.

She has told me about the first time I visited my grandparents in Copenhagen. I was still a baby, and my mother thought the food that my grandmother cooked—Austro-Hungarian desserts and meat dishes—was too heavy for my digestion. So she went to the supermarket and bought vegetables that she planned to prepare specially for me. When my grandmother found out, said my mother, her feelings were badly hurt. She didn't say a word all day to this person her son had married, a woman who obviously thought the food she had gone to such trouble to cook wasn't good enough. My grandfather finally sorted things out—and I bet he'd had practice at it. He went for a walk with my mother, she says, and tried to explain his wife's behaviour. She was sometimes difficult, he told my mother, but that was because she wanted to make everything especially nice for everyone. If I know the participants in this incident, it will have been my mother who ended up apologising.

I loved and admired my grandmother with great affection. I hoped, by some miracle, to become like her one day, at least physically, and I looked for links between us, things that we could share. When I was about fourteen and my main hobby was having crushes on supermodels, I asked my grandmother to cut out everything she could find in Danish magazines that had the slightest thing to do with Renée Simonsen, a top Danish model with eyes wide apart and a clear-cut, angular face. And my grandmother didn't laugh at me, but asked: What did you say her name was? Wait a minute, I'll get a pen—and a few weeks later the post brought the first of several envelopes full of original Danish press cuttings about Renée Simonsen.

Later, after my grandmother was dead, I began smoking, and I think I did that mainly in her memory. I chain-smoked just as she had. And I smelled just like her. And it was a long time before I gave up, because it would have felt like a betrayal. As long as I smoked, I thought, I'd be near her. But one day I quit smoking nevertheless. The fear of wrinkles was stronger.

‡

By now my grandmother has been all through the living room tidying up. She has straightened the books in the bookcase, plumped up the cushions on the sofa, removed three dead flies from between the double-glazed windows, and wondered yet again how they got there. It is always a puzzle to her, because the windows are kept closed, and when the room is aired it is through the door to the terrace. She has finally changed the bulb in the ceiling light that failed months ago; she has put the remote control back on the TV set and cleaned the screen with an anti-static cloth, which then went into the bag of rubbish. She has found a hair-slide under the chest of drawers; she has no idea whose it is or how long it has been there. And down the back of the sofa, she has finally come across the cable of her portable CD player, after she turned the whole house upside down in search of it a few weeks ago.

Now and then she gave exercise classes to the elderly on a Wednesday. They were organised by the adult education centre and took place in the multipurpose hall, where there were thick blue mats stacked against the walls and your shoes squeaked on the wooden floor. The class was called Jazzdance For Seniors, but it wasn't really much more than doing knee-bends and walking around in circles to the lively music that she played on her CD player. Recently, when she couldn't find the cable, she'd had to take her old cassette recorder, and as she was almost always late for the class she just played whatever cassette was already in it. The class had been obliged to do exercises for an hour to the accompaniment of Smetana.

The fee just covered her expenses, and she ran the class mainly for fun. She liked getting out of the house to practise her profession, even if she was acting as a carer for senior citizens rather than a physiotherapist here, as she sometimes thought when she heard the way the elderly participants were panting for breath at only the second exercise, and saw their reddened faces. She despised old age when it was obvious—protuberant veins, liver spots spreading, slack and shrivelled skin. While she called out in time to the movements in Danish, and kept reminding her group in kindly tones not to forget to breathe out, her thoughts were savage. She was affronted by the sight of most of her charges; she saw rolls of fat around the hips as a sign of inadequate self-discipline, and she thought loose folds of skin under the chin were down-right stupid. You could get something done about that these days, and she didn't know why you wouldn't do it. If her face became aesthetically unacceptable she would have a facelift. For some time she had been reading everything printed in the papers about facelifts. But on the whole she was still content with herself. She had good genes. She ate moderately. And of course she had had her varicose veins removed.

My grandmother rolls up the CD cable and puts it on the table-top. When Pista wakes up she will ask him where she should put it. He is in charge of the electrical devices; their areas of responsibility are clearly divided. A brief glance at him—he is still asleep. His head has sunk a little further to one side, he doesn't look comfortable, but he seems peaceful. Poor man, now she will have to use the vacuum cleaner, she has done everything else. She plugs it into an empty socket, pauses for a moment—and then presses the switch. The vacuum cleaner comes to life, humming loudly.

When she next looks at my grandfather, his head has turned to the other side.

‡

Budapest, May 1945. The city was in ruins, the chain bridge hung down into the Danube, broken apart, but the war was over, and with it the necessity for my grandmother to hide. She moved back to the apartment on the Oktogon, which was intact except for broken windowpanes. A girlfriend who played the piano in a bar in the evenings and who, according to Erszi, was a gifted entertainer, moved in with her. To earn money my grandmother, who spoke almost perfect French and Danish as well as Hungarian, worked as an interpreter and tourist guide in the daytime, and as a waitress in the bar where her friend played the piano in the evenings. She was given many tips, especially by Americans, says Erzsi, looking as conspiratorial as if they had tucked the money into her bra. Her earnings meant she could pay the girl who looked after my father, who was only a few months old.

My grandmother was twenty-five at this time. A beautiful young woman whose life had been interrupted by a war when it should only just have been beginning. She was alive, but everything was wrong for her. Her parents were dead, and where was her husband? POWs and people liberated from concentration camps were returning to Budapest, but there was no news of my grandfather. With every day that he failed to turn up it became less likely that he was still alive. May came, then June, then July.

Erzsi says that she first heard my grandmother speak of suicide at this time. She had told her, says Erzsi, that if Pista did not come back she would take her own life. In spite of her child? Taking her child with her? How seriously did she mean it at the time?

I remember a quotation from Nietzsche that I once heard in a religious instruction lesson at school, or an ethics class, and never found anywhere later. Or it could have been Sartre. The gist of it was that at any point in life there are always just three possibilities: you can do something, you can do nothing, or you can kill yourself. Is that an idea to give one strength? Because it makes everything, even bad times, seem to be a free choice? Did the idea of determining her own end make my grandmother feel better? Did it give her the certainty that she would never again be at anyone's mercy? Did it make her free of the worst fears—after all, you don't have to endure the unendurable: sickness, the advent of old age, frailty?

On 4 May 1945 Gunskirchen was liberated by the Americans. On the internet, I read eye-witness accounts by American soldiers. They speak of thousands of skeletally thin men, half crazed with hunger and thirst, too weak to clear away the dead lying and decaying every few metres. It was a hot May, the stench, I read, was terrible. Two days before the liberation the SS had left the camp, and in those two days alone an estimated 2000 people died. A typhus epidemic had broken out, and my grandfather was among the sick for whom there was no medicine, no food, no water. As far as we know my grandfather lay ill for a while longer, and only then did he set out for home. Again as far as we know, on foot. He reached Budapest on 10 July. It was my uncle's

birthday, Uncle István, who now lives in Melbourne. He
still remembers the day perfectly, or at least he remembers
his memory of it (he was three years old that day). The
table had been laid for his party, and there was a place laid for
my grandfather too, just in case he came back after all. And
then, sure enough, there was a knock at the door, or
the doorbell rang. They opened the door, and outside
stood my grandfather, emaciated and with a long beard,
barely recognisable, but he was alive, he was there, he was
back again.

‡

My grandmother stands in the bedroom in front of the wardrobe, thinking. She has just written her friend Erzsi a letter
that made her cry herself. She had meant to be very down-to-
earth about it, as she is with everything today, a day like any
other, one of those Sundays when you get things done. But
then she wrote 'Don't forget me' and once those three words
were set down on the sheet of paper by her fountain pen, in
handwriting that slanted to the right, she could think of no
other way to sign off, and then her eyes were suddenly
watering, she couldn't keep the tears back, and they had run
down her cheeks. Luckily Pista hadn't seen. The sound of his
regular snoring could be heard even in the kitchen. Don't
forget me—no, she didn't want Erzsi to forget her, any more

than she would have forgotten Erzsi if it had been the other way around. Erzsi, her little friend Erzsi, the only person since her schooldays to be close to her except, of course, Pista, but that was different.

She signed the letter, and just as she was going to put it in an envelope it struck her that it would be nice to send something to Erzsi's daughter Klarí. What would she like? This question finally led my grandmother, after deciding that it was too complicated to send a relatively new bottle of scent, into the bedroom to examine her wardrobe. Would the red knitted jacket that Pista had once bought her in Paris suit Klarí? No, she decides, too elegant. The same really applies to almost everything in the wardrobe, because you could call Klarí all sorts of things, but certainly not elegant— in the end my grandmother takes a pair of turquoise jogging pants out of the bottom of the wardrobe from among several folded items of clothing. They're as good as new. Hardly ever worn. And Klarí looks as if some kind of sporting activity would do her good, thinks my grandmother. She inspects the pants closely and, on finding no large marks or holes, goes in search of an envelope large enough to fit them.

‡

'Stingy'—that's the English word that Erzsi uses. I have to look it up: mean, avaricious, petty. Her daughter Klarí has joined us, has sat down beside her mother who strangely, perhaps because she uses so much lipstick, looks much younger than her daughter. Klarí wears no make-up at all. (NB to myself: keep slapping on the lipstick after the age of eighty.) The two of them laugh as they tell me about the jogging pants that my grandmother sent Klarí. Such a shabby present, they laugh, a used pair of tracksuit bottoms already threadbare at the knees.

The two women on the sofa are so amused by my grandmother's penny-pinching that I am beginning to feel uneasy. After all, she's dead. And she's my grandmother. But I know what they mean. She would get my parents to send her family-sized packs of 'Nur 1 Tropfen' brand mouthwash—'Only One Drop'—because it was cheaper than any mouthwash she could buy in Denmark. Anyone going on a journey by air had to buy her ten packets of Prince Denmark cigarettes in the duty-free shop. And Erzsi tells me that my grandmother asked her to send sewing needles from America. Sewing needles! What would they have cost here?

My father says that saving was her hobby. A positive passion. It gave her great satisfaction to find things in second-hand shops that looked new. She was the one in charge of the family finances. My grandfather gave her all that he earned, and then if he wanted to buy her a birthday present he had to ask her for a sum of money and the permission to spend it.

We all felt the force of her thrift. Her presents were always received apprehensively: what were we not going to be pleased to get this time? I remember T-shirts much too small for me, and you knew from the smell of them that they had been in my grandparents' house for a long time (in fact they smelled as if they had been stored in an ashtray). A book that looked as if it had been read. A bottle not quite full of bath foam. And my grandmother always asked questions. Had we been pleased, had we hung the picture yet? And next time she came to visit, she would want to see it. Even when, for once, you really had been pleased with something, you felt as if you had to pretend you were pleased, because a 'Thank you so much' was never enough for her, even if you really meant it, and as soon as the opportunity arose she twisted the words in your mouth—she was a mistress of that art. 'Do you like it?'—'Yes, very much.'—'Will you wear it?'—'Yes, of course.'—'I'd like to see what you look like in it, so send a photo.'—'Yes, I will.'—'You're sure the sleeves aren't too tight?'—'Not at all, it fits perfectly.'—'And you don't already have one like it?'—'No, I don't.'—'So why don't you have one like it already, don't you like velour sweaters?'—'Oh, I do, I think velour sweaters are very attractive, thank you so much.' And so on, and so forth.

I meet Erzsi on two consecutive mornings. Our conversations seem to tire her; the longer we talk, the longer are the pauses in which I am never sure if she is just thinking, or if something else will follow. 'You have to ask me something,' she tells me several times. The filter tips of the cigarettes stubbed out in the ashtray are red with her lipstick.

What kind of woman was my grandmother?

'She had two personalities,' says Erzsi. 'One was very formal. The traditional feminine image. Perfect behaviour, addressing her husband formally, not officially communist or Jewish, model children. All things considered a great success. I was the only person who saw the other side of her. Then she was silly. We laughed a lot, and she acted like a teenager. Relaxed. Amusing. We talked about anything and everything, absolutely everything. When we met we had a drink at breakfast, strong spirits, slivovitz or something like that. But...' She scrutinises me as if to make sure that I can bear the truth. 'She wasn't a happy woman. Deep down inside she was very insecure. She thought nobody liked her. It was her *idée fixe*. She thought no one in the world liked her. No one but Pista.'

I am surprised. That would never have occurred to me. I try to reconcile what Erzsi says with my own picture of my grandmother. The doctor's beautiful wife, the successful mother, the elegant hostess, the excellent cook, amusing company at table, this interesting, clever, temperamental woman, sometimes appearing to be arrogant—can she really have been profoundly insecure? Can she have felt unloved and lonely?

As the English phrase goes, it does ring a bell.

The deepest feeling known to me is the sense of not belonging. I grew up with that feeling. It is not a pleasant one, and I don't know where it comes from. Ever since I can remember I have felt as if I were in the way. As if everyone would be happier without me, and I don't mean just my family but my friends as well, in fact everyone, always. I feel as if I don't really fit in. As if everyone else was round and I was square, or vice versa. No one loves me, no one *can* love me. That is my deepest conviction and at the same time my greatest fear, and if I follow the idea to the end it leads me to the feeling more familiar to me than any other: I am all alone.

It is as if Erzsi had given me a treasure. What extraordinary news—my grandmother felt just like me?

I'd like to call everyone I know, here and now, and tell them: I'm not crazy after all. I'm only my grandmother's granddaughter. She had it too. She was like me. I am like her. Hurrah. I could hug Erzsi, I would like to pick her right up, that frail little woman, and dance around the room with her. I don't do it. I'm too overwhelmed by this new realisation, it moves my deepest feelings so much. And perhaps she wouldn't like to be picked up. So I sit still and act as if nothing had happened.

And suddenly I also understand my grandmother's love, which was so exclusive, so needy, so great, and ultimately conditional. Prove that I am wrong, prove that I am worth loving, and then I will always be with you, I will follow you even into death.

Suddenly I can also imagine why she didn't want to live without him, why she died with him.

‡

My grandmother is standing in the kitchen, her apron still tied around her waist, searching the groceries cupboard for a sachet of dried yeast. She is perfectly sure that she still has some, or perhaps she isn't quite so sure after all, it's quite a long time since she last did any baking, but she always keeps some, so it must be somewhere—ah, here, no, that's vanilla sugar. Maybe in the drawer with the baking sheets? She pulls out the drawer under the refrigerator—suddenly there is a loud bang in the next room. Then my grandfather's voice swearing in Hungarian. So he's woken up. My grandmother goes into the next room, with the dog following her at a prudent distance.

My grandfather is standing beside the piano, with a pile

of sheet music on the floor in front of him. It must have fallen off the top where it had been stacked. 'I don't know how it happened either,' he says apologetically, but the annoyance he expects goes unexpressed. 'Shit happens,' says my grand-mother in English, picking up the sheet music. She might also have said 'Tel Aviv', her second favourite such saying, a distortion of *C'est la vie*. Apart from the 'Tel Aviv' comment, her sense of humour is largely limited to listening equably to my grandfather's jokes for the hundredth time. She puts the sheet music back on the piano. 'You'll have to get dressed if you want to come with me,' she says. 'I put out a shirt and a pair of trousers for you.' Then she goes back into the kitchen with the dog behind her.

She does indeed find a whole packet of dried yeast sachets in the drawer with the baking sheets. 'Well, look at that!' she says out loud. She opens the fridge and takes out eggs, a packet of butter, and a litre of milk. Then she looks at the little notebook lying open on the kitchen table and reads what it says, her forefinger following her own handwriting line by line. The sound of the piano is suddenly heard from the next room. First a distorted chord. Then Chopin's Nocturne in E minor, through which you can cheat your way very nicely by clever use of the pedals. Runs blur, trills echo under the sound of held chords, a rewarding piece to play for those who don't practise regularly.

My grandmother softens butter in the *bain-marie*, breaks two eggs, separates the yolks from the whites, and roasts poppy seeds briefly in a pan before crushing them in the mortar. Since poppy seeds come under the narcotics law in Denmark, and she always has to get them at the pharmacy on a prescription which my grandfather makes out for her, she uses them sparingly. Not today. She tips more poppy seeds than the recipe calls for into the pan, and can't help smiling when it strikes her that the cake will probably turn out very tranquillising. All she has forgotten is an unwaxed lemon, so she uses a treated one instead. It's not going to poison anyone, she thinks, grating the peel expertly. Then she tips the contents of the sachet of dried yeast into a bowl, adds water and sugar, and stirs it.

Next door, my grandfather has just stumbled through the same run for the fourth time. 'Go on, please!' my grandmother calls from the kitchen. 'We know that bit already.' She offers the dog a spoon with a little of the mixture still on it. 'Mmm,' she says. 'Delicious.' The dog cautiously sniffs the spoon and prefers not to taste it. All of a sudden the chords of Mendelssohn's Wedding March ring out from the living room. The piano is out of tune; it sounds like a worn-out recording.

'Pista,' calls my grandmother. She is in a good mood. It came over her quite suddenly, and now there it is.

My grandfather doesn't seem to have heard her. He goes on playing the piano undeterred, hitting a few wrong notes but sticking to the time.

'Pista!' she calls, louder this time.

The piano-playing stops.

'Yes?' he calls back.

'Love you too!' she calls.

'What did you say?' he asks.

'Love you too!' she repeats. She pours the mixture from the bowl into a mixer with dough hooks fitted, along with flour and the softened butter, and switches the mixer to maximum speed. She wants the dough to be so smooth that it comes away cleanly from the bowl. That's what her recipe says. When she switches off the mixer the piano has fallen silent. My grandfather is standing in the doorway.

'What did you say?' he asks.

A little of her cheerfulness wears off. Repeated questions bore her.

'We'll set off as soon as I've finished baking these,' she says; she doesn't feel like joking any more.

'Yes,' he says. 'Something smells good, what is it?'

'Does it smell good?' asks my grandmother. 'Maybe the poppy seeds.'

'Making beigli?'

'Yes.'

'For us?'

'For Christmas.'

'Can I have a taste?'

'Paws off!' she says, but she waits until my grandfather has dipped his forefinger in the mixture and tasted it.

'Mmm,' he says.

'There, now out you go!' My grandmother sets the temperature and fan of the oven to maximum. Now she has to work fast, she doesn't want the dough to rise at this point. She divides it into four equal portions, takes a rolling pin out of a drawer and rolls each portion out flat.

'Mucika...' My grandfather is still in the kitchen. 'Wouldn't you like to think it over again? You could spend Christmas...'

'I'm busy, can't you see that?' she interrupts him, as she looks for a wooden spoon in the drawer. Ah, there's one. She takes it, spoons up the poppyseed filling, puts a large blob on each of the rolled portions of dough and spreads it lengthwise.

'You could spend Christmas in Munich,' he says.

My grandmother takes hold of the long sides of the first portion and folds it over the filling like a Swiss roll.

'Or with Erzsi. You wouldn't be alone.'

Now the second portion.

'Stop that.' She makes it sound like a threat.

My grandfather looks at my grandmother from the doorway. Her movements are economical, nothing goes wrong, the poppyseed filling is entirely enclosed by the sides of the dough, none of it spills out. She rolls up the third portion.

'But I do think you...'

Then the fourth.

'Pista, do go and put some warm clothes on. It's much too cold for you in here. And stop all that. The answer is no.'

She looks at her recipe again. She doesn't know it by heart, because she makes this cake only once a year, normally not until November, but never mind, it will freeze well. My grandfather leaves the doorway. 'Bake for 30 to 45 minutes,' she reads, 'or until nicely browned.' She takes the oven mitts off the hook, opens the oven door, takes out a baking sheet, lines it with baking paper, places the four rolls of dough on it and puts it in the oven. She sets the timer to 30 minutes.

'Half an hour,' she calls.

'Which socks should I wear?' he calls back from the bedroom.

‡

Cut to Paris. Here, in a quiet side street off the rue de Rivoli, a distant relation of my grandmother lives—exactly how distant she herself doesn't know. Her name is Illi, and she

56

even looks a little like my grandmother, the same hooded eyelids, the same eyebrows looking as if they were painted on, the same short lashes. Illi will be ninety years old in a few days' time. She lives on the fifth floor, and there is no lift in her apartment block. She goes up and down the steep, curving staircase several times every day. It keeps her young, she says, making a face like a little girl who has said something terribly silly.

I have met her only once before, in 1990, when I spent six months in Paris. At the time I was not particularly interested in this rather odd old lady who was apparently a relation of mine. I visited her once, taking a friend with me. We sat there with Illi for about an hour, and then we left and I thought no more about her.

Illi was born in Vienna, and spent her childhood there. In the early 1930s she lived in Berlin, went to school in Charlottenburg and then, 'because of that Hitler', as she says, she moved to Budapest. She lived there from 1936 onwards.

She knew them all, my grandmother's parents, my grandfather's parents; after all, she was related to some of them. I can ask her what they were like, all those people who are only names to me.

Gizella Fellner, the melancholy Zionist, my grandmother's mother. What was *she* like?

'Giza?' asks Illi. 'She was nice, very nice. And beautiful.'

'And her husband, Elémer?

'He was a dear,' says Illi.

In answer to my further questions she tells me a little more. Gizella, who came from Croatia, never spoke Hungarian without an accent. She suffered from depression and used to see an analyst. 'He was the most important man in her life.' She was very thrifty—another one! Illi is too polite to say she was mean with money. They could have afforded fresh bread, but she always bought yesterday's left-overs at the baker's, and even cake that had gone dry; there were many jokes about that in the family circle. She wanted her daughter to be better off some day, that was what she was saving for. And her golden rule was a Hungarian proverb. 'Never mind how much you have, it's always possible to have more...never mind how good something is, it could always be better.' Illi repeats it in Hungarian too, pleased that she can still remember it.

And Elémer?

He had been the nicest person in the world. An engineer, he worked for the Hungarian railways. Everyone loved him, especially Vera, his only child. Gizella managed money so well that they could have afforded to buy a really nice apartment of their own in Budapest, but Illi doesn't remember exactly what happened, and she doesn't seem to want to search her memories any more—at any rate, she changes the subject, and instead she says something about the people who have moved into the next-door apartment here in Paris; she doesn't like them.

I am sitting on the very edge of a chair that I share with a gremlin doll the size of a baby, seated behind me and claiming the back of the chair for itself. It has oversized ears like a bat's and brown plastic feet, and I try not to touch it because, to be honest, I find it a bit disgusting. The whole apartment is crammed with dolls. Dolls in folk costumes, brightly coloured rag dolls, plastic Barbies, cuddly animal toys, characters out of comics, babushkas—there's not a corner in the place where some of them aren't sitting or standing. Arranged in order of size, they stand side by side on shelves, sit on tables and chests of drawers, look at you from window-sills and the arms of sofas. 'My darlings,' Illi calls them. There must be well over a thousand here.

During the German occupation she had very little contact with my grandmother, she tells me. She herself was hardly ever in Budapest at the time, so she doesn't know where my grandmother was hiding. 'Maybe in the cellar of the building on the Oktogon?' There is an inquiry in her voice. She does know that Gizella and Elémer were shot. At least, she nods when I mention it. But she doesn't remember how she heard about it, nor does she know any more of the details, and my grandmother never discussed it with her.

Suddenly she changes the subject.

'You know,' she says, 'once the Jews hid in the synagogue for three days, and for three days nobody knew they were in there. And then they were found; half of them were shot in the Danube, the other half were allowed to go free. Wouldn't you like another piece of chocolate? Here. I'm addicted to chocolate, did you know? I'm crazy about it. Here, do have another piece.' She pushes the chocolate bar she has already broken into over the table, which means the subject has been changed again, for the time being at least. It seems somehow familiar to me: we don't talk about these things, they're not nice to think about, and it was all so long ago.

Illi keeps standing up; she stoops slightly as she walks, but she is very quick on her feet. Each time she comes back a moment later with something else that she has fetched from a corner of her attic apartment, which is full of nooks and crannies. Another brand of chocolate. A pair of shoes that she doesn't need any more. Photos.

'Here, look, that was me two weeks ago in New York.'

She shows me photographs of herself with a young man on the Empire State Building. The young man is called Felix, and is a steward with SwissAir, she tells me. He is gay and is her 'best friend'. A little later she reads me a letter that Felix wrote her. A declaration of love for his girlfriend Lizzi, who 'loves chocolate and always wears striped stockings'. Illi laughs as she reads that aloud. 'I really do always wear striped stockings, did you know?' She stretches a leg in the air, pulling up her trouser leg a little way, and sure enough a stocking with blue and green stripes comes into view.

How did she herself survive the Holocaust?

'What, me?'

She waves the question away, as if to say: oh, that really isn't so interesting, but very well, then. 'I spent three months in England, then I came back to Budapest, and then my Papa——' (she stresses the last syllable, like Romy Schneider in *Sissi*)—'then my Papa knew the Swiss consul, and we got special Swiss passports, and they meant that no one could come into our apartment, but then we had to leave. And we went to Switzerland. My parents wanted me to take a course in banking there.' She narrows her eyes and puts her tongue out; obviously she still finds this an impossible idea. 'Me, a course in banking!'

That's how history unfolds. The Holocaust is raging, Jews are transported to Auschwitz in their hundreds and thousands to be gassed—and others know someone who can get them false passports, and they quarrel with their parents about the totally normal aspects of life.

She speaks a German that no longer really exists. It has a slight touch of Austrian, the lilting inflections of a Hotel

Sacher concierge, with emphasis on the vowels, steering straight towards every A, every O, and lingering briefly on it, an old-fashioned and affected accent, but charming too. She has Austrian turns of phrase as well, telling me how the Bösendorfer piano used to stand in their 'salon'.

My father has told me that the family always considered Illi rather peculiar. They liked her, they drank tea with her, and were relieved when she left again. A zany character who travelled the world instead of having children, and managed to live in Paris without letting that city lend her the faintest touch of elegance.

Did she know that my grandfather was in Mauthausen?

'Where?'

In Mauthausen, in the concentration camp there.

'All I remember is that he was in the war...in Korea.'

Yes, but that was much later.

'Later, yes.'

No, I mean the Second World War.

There is a pause. I wouldn't like to force a conversation that she doesn't want on her. Perhaps you live a longer, happier life if you don't look back so much. And perhaps she really doesn't know much about it either.

I would have loved to ask her what my grandmother was like as a young woman, what life was like for Jews under communism—now that I am here, I realise that I shall not get the answers I had hoped for from her. My grandmother had been so beautiful, she says, several times, so beautiful. My great-grandparents were such dears. The end was a shock. By 'the end' she means the death of my grandparents. She tells me that she sometimes used to play cards with my grandmother until late into the night. Rummy. They played for money, she tells me. She laughs. But she would rather talk about Felix the air steward; she is planning to travel to Oman with him next.

I go back in time once more. How long did she live in Berlin, I ask?

'We left in 1936. Listen, I know a joke. It dates from those days. A Jewish family wants to employ a new household help. A woman comes along, and they tell her straight out, we are very sorry, but we have to tell you that you would be working for a Jewish family here. And the household help says: Jewish or not Jewish, I don't mind one way or the other, just so long as you're Aryan.' She laughs. 'But is it any better in Germany now?' she asks, suddenly serious.

The situation for Jews?

'Yes?'

Well, compared with 1936 some things have certainly improved, I say. And she is already changing the subject again.

‡

If I had to divide up the story of my grandparents' lives into sections, the first long chapter would conclude with the end of the Second World War. The next would be headed 'Communism', and would cover the years 1945 to 1956. I don't know much about those years. Hungary turning into a socialist state, the Warsaw Pact, the Iron Curtain, it's as vague as that in my mind. My grandparents would probably have told me something about it, just for once, if I had asked them, but I never did ask. They lived in Hungary, that was all. He was a doctor, she was a physiotherapist, my father was a little boy, my aunt was a little girl. They lived in an apartment, they went on holiday in summer, and they went to bed in the evening. What else of any importance should I have asked?

There's a woman called Julia, known as Julika, who lives in Zürich and who was friends with my grandparents in the early fifties. Her first husband, Tamás, whom she divorced in the mid-fifties, was a childhood friend of my grandmother's. Maybe he even once had a relationship with her, Julika tells me on the phone, she doesn't know, it didn't interest her, because if there ever had been anything between them it was over long before Julika met her husband and my grandmother met my grandfather. Together with another married couple they formed a small circle of friends in Budapest, a clique of three families. They lived only five minutes' walk away from each other in the city centre, close to the Opera House. All three husbands were in some branch of medicine—a dentist, a general practitioner, an orthopaedic surgeon—and each couple had two small children of about the same age. All three husbands were also members of the Communist Party.

I ask her whether she thinks my grandfather had been a committed communist.

'Heavens, no,' she says. No one, she adds, believed in such ideals, 'or at least not in those circles.' You joined the Party out of sheer opportunism, because that gave you a hope of getting work and living in safety.

I ask her whether the fact that all three couples were Jewish had anything to do with their friendship. I had read that even after the end of the German occupation, Jews were considered second-class citizens in Hungary.

'Well, you know,' she says, 'we never talked about these things. We all had our own stories. Today they always make such a drama of it if someone's been raped. I was pregnant at the time, and it showed, and they took care not to harm the baby. There was nothing I could do about it. There were no witnesses. We avoided talking about such subjects at the time. As far as we were concerned, life began in 1945.'

Was that new life a good one?

'Yes,' she says. 'We were all right.' She tells me that they often went for outings at that time. All the three families had cars, elegant cars, she says, not many Hungarians could afford cars like that, and they used to drive out into the country. And when they wanted to go to a café for lunch, they were often told that unfortunately there was nothing the café owners could offer them, not even eggs. 'We always said how terribly poor people were in the country,' she tells me, 'not even eggs to eat, how tragic.' Only much later, a few years ago, did the suspicion dawn on her that there were probably plenty of eggs available, but the café staff just didn't want to serve them, obvious Party members that they were, putting on such airs and graces with their expensive cars and pretty children and good clothes.

'We were naïve,' she says, 'we women in particular took no interest at all in politics.' She remembers only one time when anyone at all of their acquaintance spoke in negative terms of the communists. A German architect who was involved in the building of the new Interior Ministry. He said, she tells me, that the government had had an opening straight into the Danube built into the basement storey of the building, through which torture victims could be disposed of leaving no trace. She had been surprised at the time, she says, that he spoke so openly, but she thought no more about it.

So she doesn't know, I ask, what my grandparents' political ideas were like?

'There was a joke going the rounds at the time. "Two Hungarians meet. One tells the other, I'm off to the Institute of Seeing and Hearing now. Oh yes, says the other, and what may that be? And the first replies: well, I hope they can help me there, because I don't see the things that I hear."'

That made them laugh in Budapest at the time.

‡

This is what my father has told me about his Hungarian childhood:

The apartment on the Oktogon had five large rooms, heated by stoves. There was a balcony or a walkway in the open air by which you reached the inner courtyard. I don't quite understand exactly how it connected with the apartment, but anyway, you got to it from the kitchen, and it was not roofed over. My grandfather had fitted out one of the rooms as his consulting room. He was a consultant at the Budapest János Kóház (St John's Hospital), and many patients from the country came to see him privately. They paid in kind, so there were usually a few chickens and rabbits living in the little inner courtyard.

My father doesn't remember whether my grandmother was working too, or what she did all day—maybe she went shopping, he says. What, every day? Illi thinks that, of course, my grandmother was working as a physiotherapist and also as an interpreter and tourist guide at weekends—'she knew French and German so well.'

They had a nursemaid who came in every day for the children, and a cook who lived with them and who also did the laundry in the laundry room in the basement. My father says that nursemaids were normal in Budapest at the time, all families had one. But a childhood friend of my aunt, who by coincidence also lives in Munich now, doesn't agree. Not all families in Budapest had a nursemaid, not by any means, or a cook either. She, for instance, grew up without any domestic staff at home, and her father was a highly regarded architect. ('Oh yes?' is all my father says when I tell him this.)

My father remembers summer holidays in Csillaghegy, a little bathing resort near Budapest where families could spend the summer months comfortably. It was a fenced-in socialist holiday paradise, where children ran about unsupervised in swimming trunks, their mothers met at the swimming pool, and the fathers came by train to visit at weekends or in the evenings after work.

My grandfather had a DKW car, a big, black vehicle. He had had an Adler before that, so Erzsi's daughter Klarí told me. He was the first person she knew who drove a car. At the time all Budapest got about on foot or by tram, and the trams were always so crowded that people even rode on the outside, hanging on.

Really close friends of my grandparents might drop in unannounced in the evening. Then they played cards until late at night, my father remembers, only the grown-ups, of course.

Twice a week my grandmother took him skating. She sat in the spectators' seats at the ice rink, freezing, while he learned to skate backwards and turn pirouettes. They didn't do that for fun, says my father, but to enable him to travel later—'so that their children would have a future.' Top sporting personalities were allowed to travel out of Hungary. After a while they had both had enough of skating; they tried fencing instead. Eventually they gave that up too.

My father remembers his grandparents, my grandfather's parents. Their names were Frida and Sándor, and they lived five minutes' walk from the Oktogon, on the busy Lenin Ring, which a few years earlier had still been the Elisabeth Ring. Sándor's bookshop was on the ground floor of the building. He was ill for a long time, says my father, and was always lying in bed in a darkened room. When he died in 1949 my father was five years old, so it's hard to know exactly what he understood as 'a long time'. Sándor's wife Frida owned a dance school, which was very progressive for a woman at the time. Her school was known all over Budapest, and to this day my father is still addressed by Hungarians whom she taught to dance when they were children. She was known as Tánci-Néni, Dance-Auntie. She was small and sturdy, and my father describes her as self-opinionated and egotistic—a memory that could have been influenced by my grandmother, who couldn't stand her mother-in-law. The feeling was mutual.

There is a photograph of my great-grandparents taken in New York in 1928, in North Manhattan, Riverside Drive, corner of 223rd Street. The statue of a Hungarian freedom fighter, Lajos Kossuth, was unveiled there that day. It seems to have been a great occasion—Frida and Sándor came by ship to America specially. They are posing in the photograph as if the national anthem were just being played: small, stocky Frida, chin held high, one foot gracefully placed in front of the other as befits the owner of a school of dance. Beside her is Sándor, looking as dignified as if his own statue were being unveiled. He stands very upright, hands by his thighs, a cravat tucked into his dark blazer, the bookseller of the Elisabeth Ring who had come to the other end of the world to express his love of his fatherland.

Would they be glad to know they had a great-granddaughter going right across New York to have herself photographed in front of this statue? More likely, perhaps, they'd be surprised. It's a Sunday morning in January. While every normal person

70

is still in bed, or just wondering whether to go to a café for breakfast, I'm setting out. I have to go all through the city, which not only takes a ridiculously long time, but is also incredibly cold, because the subway is draughty, and in addition I get out one station too soon and have to walk several blocks against the icy wind. I contemplate turning back several times on the way. But I somehow feel it is my duty to go on. Block after block after block.

I recognise the statue from afar. It is very ugly: a man with a long coat standing on a plinth with two more figures at his feet, a soldier and an old man. *Kossuth*, says the inscription in large letters, *the great champion of liberty*. I know it from the photograph with my great-grandparents, and from another photograph with my grandparents who had their own picture taken here in 1982. And I have been here once before myself, in 1990, with my father. But that was on a warm day, as you can tell from the photo we took of ourselves in front of the statue with the delayed action shutter release. I am wearing a T-shirt and sunglasses with small, round lenses which no one had told me really didn't suit me.

Today I have a thick winter jacket on, and a cap which I can say for myself doesn't suit me, but never mind that, it's warm. I don't know how the delayed release works on my camera, so I ask a passer-by if he'd be kind enough to take a photo of me in front of the statue. His glance travels from me to the statue and back again. 'Sorry,' he says, 'I'd rather not.' He walks on, and I can understand him. He must think I'm some kind of nationalistic nutcase. The next man to come along is kind enough to take the photo. In the picture he took I do look like a nationalistic nutcase, with a mad grin on my face and the cast-iron figure of a soldier next to me. Anyway, my father likes it when I email it to him.

‡

My father and my aunt often asked my grandfather to write his memoirs. That way, they hoped, they might learn something about all the events he never mentioned, particularly the time he spent in the concentration camp, which they may have imagined—for they knew nothing about it—as worse than it really was. And one day, when they had long ago given up expecting that he would, on 23 July 1986, he actually did sit down and began writing.

'You have asked me so often to write about my life that today, on my seventy-seventh birthday, I am sitting down to try to satisfy your curiosity.' So begins his account, which amounts in all to seven and a half closely written A5 pages. He wrote in fountain pen on a notepad advertising a company making medical instruments, and curiously enough he wrote in German.

'I was born on 23 July 1909 in Zalaegerszeg, a small town in western Hungary. My parents and grandparents never lived there. The reason for this important incident in my life is as follows: Mother's best friend, Dr Malvin Kovács, one of the first women doctors in Hungary, lived there and was going to help Mother with the birth. She was the same doctor who performed the ceremony that Jewish boys, according to the ritual prescriptions, otherwise have to undergo at the hands of a slaughterer: it was a small operation, probably performed without anaesthetic.'

Why did he choose to write this memoir in German? He had learnt the language at school, and perfected it during his studies of medicine. Because of the strict Hungarian laws affecting Jews, he qualified in Vienna. His German was rather formal, and sometimes sounded like a literal translation from a foreign language, which perhaps it was. Now and then he confused grammatical case endings, or made up his own version of a verb, for instance saying *parkieren* instead of *parken* for parking a car—it sounded old-fashioned and as if it came from another world.

He did not get very far with his memoir. His account ends in the middle of a subordinate clause, and he hasn't even gone to school yet. What he did write consists mainly of a list of all his relations. His parents, grandparents and great-grandparents are introduced in detail, but so are first cousins

73

and second cousins, with their names, professions and characters, along with a few spinster aunts and a ping-pong champion, the product of an uncle's liaison with his housekeeper.

And yet his memoir tells us more about him than he ever told us himself. For it is a Jewish family history through and through. His father's bookshop was seized under the Jewish laws of the Nazi period; two cousins died doing the forced labour incumbent on Jewish men; several members of the family were gassed at Auschwitz. His mother's maiden name was Mayersberg, and her family could boast the leaders of several Jewish communities among its members. Now and then in his memoir he suddenly launches into a long paragraph about the history of the Jews in Hungary. ('The Kazars were an Asiatic tribe of the Jewish religion, and had come to Hungary during the great migration of peoples even before they conquered the Carpathian country in the year 895...')

And he writes that he comes from a family who felt that they were Hungarians of Jewish origin. A family of assimilated Jews. His own father had never observed a Seder evening, he writes, and then explains what that is: 'It is the festival on which Jewish families gather at the home of the eldest for supper, to celebrate in songs, stories, and with special ceremonies the liberation of the Jews from slavery in Egypt, and it is held every year at Pessach, Easter.' Obviously he assumes that his children, then both around forty years old, have never heard of a Seder evening. On his seventy-seventh birthday, then, he tells them something about Jewish tradition for the first time, the tradition of his family, if only in written form. He kept them entirely out of that area of his life, which obviously meant so much more than he led us to believe.

If I am to be perfectly honest, that makes me not only sad but even a little angry. For he stole a part of my identity as well, deprived me of an essential part of my sense of self, bequeathed me a gap in my identity that seems like a mystery. I lack a piece of myself. Something is missing, and I don't even know exactly what.

Such a pity for something to disappear.

‡

Back to Paris again. A friend of my grandmother's, Hélène, lives in the 16th arrondissement. She is ninety-four years old, with an immaculate hairstyle. Her hair, the colour of autumn leaves, is teased on top of her head and worn in a chignon at the back. Her lips are painted coral red, and at first I take her gigantic tinted horn-rimmed glasses to be an expression of eccentric taste. Only when she mentions in passing that she can see almost nothing these days do I realise that they are in fact to help her vision.

Hélène and her husband, who died in 1983, knew my grandparents very well. They met in 1949 at a medical congress in Budapest. French communist doctors exchanged views with Hungarian communist doctors, and since it was all very friendly, wives were allowed to join them in the evenings. It was pure chance that they sat at the same table, my grandparents and the French medical couple—he was an endocrinologist, she was a psychotherapist—Hélène says they made friends at once. 'We just clicked,' she says. '*Tout était clair.*'

Hélène and her husband saw to it that my grandmother was appointed their official interpreter for the duration of their visit to Budapest. Whenever there was something to be seen in the city, or a lecture to be interpreted, my grandmother translated for them. The wives liked each other, and the husbands liked each other, and yes, they just clicked.

Perhaps, for my grandparents, they personified the wide world that, seen from Hungary at that time, probably looked even wider than it really is. At the end of 1949 my grandfather was able to travel to France. With the permission of the Communist Party, or at its wish, he went as *Assistant étranger de la Faculté de Médecine de Paris*. A whole year of further training. Did he have to spend a long time discussing it with my grandmother? Or did it seem a good idea at once? Anyway, they decided that my grandmother would go with him, at least for part of the time. She spent six months in all with my grandfather in Paris. Half a year without the children, whom she left at home in Budapest in the care of the nursemaid. My father was five, my aunt was two years old. And if they had not both fallen ill with polio, my grandmother would have stayed away even longer. I don't know any woman now with small children who would go away without them for six months. But then nor do I know any woman who is still under thirty and has survived a war. Her hunger for life, for beauty, for brilliance was probably greater than I can imagine.

Hélène lives in a small neo-classical building that looks as if it had been under a preservation order for at least a hundred years. Wherever you look you see ornamental furniture, floral decoration, porcelain plates—the wallpaper is silk, the cupboards old and decorated with intarsia work. Sounds of cooking can be heard from the kitchen, which is next to the living room, the lid of a pan clatters, an extractor hood is switched on. A little later the maid will serve the meal. There will be four courses for 'Madame Hélène' and her guest, not counting the final chocolate cake.

Hélène talks fast and at length, and laughs loudest of all at herself. She wears an elegant blouse, snakeskin shoes with bows on them, and her lipstick doesn't vanish into thin air until just before the last course. I can see why my grandmother liked her. This woman was her equal. Few women of Hélène's age can wear enormous tinted glasses like that so naturally, or collect remnants of food in her mouth and spit them out on the plate without batting an eyelid, never mind interrupting her own flow of talk.

Beside her telephone, an old-fashioned set with a dial and a cable, stands a framed photograph of my grandparents. I know it. It was taken when they were on a cruise in the North Sea a few years before their death. They look as if they could have been dining at the captain's table at the time. My grandfather is in a white dinner jacket, my grandmother wears gold jewellery with her grey silk dress. She has a green ribbon around her waist, and she is smiling radiantly at her husband from the side, just as she looks at him in their wedding photograph.

'I think of them every day,' says Hélène, when she notices that I am looking at the photo. And then she says she blames herself dreadfully for not telling my grandmother that she could come and live with her when my grandfather died. She had often meant to say so, she had intended to say that in every telephone conversation. But my grandfather had always been there in the background, so that they could never speak freely. 'And then it was too late.' After a short pause, she says, 'Vera was so frightened of being alone after Pista's death. Particularly in Denmark.'

Surtout au Danemark? Did my grandmother end up not liking Denmark so much after all? Did she complain to her chic French friend about the Danes? I can imagine that. But would the prospect of a room in the 16th arrondissement have deterred her from coming to her decision? I doubt it.

How did she, Hélène, see my grandparents?

'Vera was very beautiful,' she says. That is what obviously struck everyone about her first. 'She was more extrovert than Pista, she talked more. He wouldn't let you get very close to him. Perhaps that was to do with his experiences.'

What experiences does she mean, exactly?

'Mauthausen, he was in the concentration camp.'

Did he talk about it?

'He talked about it, yes. No details, of course. But he said he was there.'

When did he talk about it?

'Oh, right away. When we met.'

On the very first evening?

'Yes, I think so.'

That's unusual, he would never usually mention the subject.

'We told each other everything. We had so much in common. We'd all just been through a bad time. Vera had lost her parents, my father died in Auschwitz.'

They said they were Jewish?

'Of course.'

On the very first evening?

'Yes.'

Just as Hélène had said at first, *tout était clair*, it was all clear. They happened to be sitting at the same table, two married couples, both Jewish, who had only very recently escaped death by the skin of their teeth, all of them, in Hungary, Austria, France. Was that the bond they had in common? Was that why it was all clear? Because they were Jews—European Jews?

‡

Once, over supper, I watched a TV documentary about Hitler on the Obersalzberg with my parents and grandparents. This was around 1989 or 1990. My grandparents were staying with us in Munich, and it was one of those *Spiegel TV* reports that like to show newly discovered historical material illustrating the subject in pictures. This time the sensation was that filmed footage from the Obersalzberg, some of it taken by Eva Braun, had been coloured in afterwards. You could see Hitler hugging his German shepherd dog, Eva Braun turning a cartwheel, and the children of assorted Nazis sitting on the terrace eating ice-creams. I thought it was all very interesting. So that was how these people had lived, how they looked in colour. At last, I thought, it's easier to imagine it all; you realised that these things had happened in the same century as the one in which we were still living.

My grandparents didn't say a word all through the program. I was sitting at the front of the room, quite close to the TV set, and didn't venture to turn round and look at them. I felt somehow reluctant to do so. I didn't know what they would think of the pictures, but as they stayed sitting there, and no one switched channels, I supposed that they too were interested. When the program was over I was the first to speak. 'Interesting, don't you think?' I said in as neutral a tone as possible as the final credits came up, turning to look at the others with a neutral expression on my face. 'You think so?' said my grandmother. 'I don't. Why would anyone be interested in what Hitler was like in private?' She stood up, collected the plates, and went into the kitchen. My grandfather said nothing, and I felt ashamed.

‡

Like so many Jewish stories, the story of my father's family is of a hopeless attempt to fit in. My grandfather's father, the owner of the bookshop on the Elisabeth Ring, was born Samuel Adler. But because German names in Hungary suggested that their bearers were Jewish, he decided—to be on the safe side—to make the name more Hungarian. Samuel became Sándor, Adler became Adorján. My grandmother had herself baptised after the war, along with her children, and officially became a Protestant—a Protestant atheist, to be precise. (She might just as easily have become a Catholic, but the Evangelical church happened to be closer.) My grandfather never officially converted from Judaism, although it is not clear, even to the highest authorities, whether it is actually possible to stop being a Jew. And if it is, whether that is true to oneself.

Probably not, I guess.

My grandparents acted as if they were not at all interested in their own Jewish identity, but they showed a lively interest in that of other people. My aunt has told me that my grandparents often used to discuss between themselves whether someone was Jewish, and thus one of their own kind. Is such and such a person one of the *nostras*, they would wonder; it was their code for saying, is he one of us? As if you could tell by looking at people that they are Jewish. As if you could smell it.

My aunt has also told me how my grandparents reacted when they learned that my father had fallen in love with my mother. Over supper they had wondered, at length, what her father had done in the war, whether he had been a Nazi or not. Later, when they met my mother's parents, and the two grandfathers played piano duets in Heidelberg, they came to the conclusion that it was probably all okay. But did my father really have to go and fall in love with a German girl?

Once, when I was in Israel with my parents and my

brothers—this was in 1994—my father was asked by a security official at the airport as we were flying out again whether he was Jewish—the names of his children, Johanna, Dávid, Gabriel, all of Hebrew origin, suggested it. To the surprise of us all, my father said he didn't know. His mother had so often impressed it upon him that being Jewish was deadly dangerous that he preferred to be cautious about admitting it, even in Israel.

‡

I recently flew to Israel with an Israeli airline, and on boarding the plane saw that most of the passengers were already seated; Berlin was probably only a stopover on their flight. Many of the men wore kippahs on their heads, and so did the red-haired American in the seat next to me, whom I liked at once, although our entire conversation throughout the flight consisted of no more than 'excuse me', and, 'thank you'. The passengers came from all over the world. I heard English, Italian, French and Russian spoken. No one took any notice of me, I knew no one, and yet I felt curiously at ease. Unbidden, a sentence formed in my head: Ah, here you all are!

It is odd, indeed inexplicable, but among these strangers who were all probably Jews, or at least most of them, I felt at home. That feeling did not leave me even after we landed, and was to accompany me for the next few days. In the middle of what is probably the least secure country in the world, I felt oddly safe. Calm. Much calmer than usual. Ah, here you all are, I thought, and I felt at home. In a country with a climate that does not suit me, whose language I do not speak, and whose script I cannot read.

On the flight back I was surrounded by elderly Israeli married couples. I do not understand Hebrew, so I don't know what they said to each other, but all the time, in fact for the whole five-hour flight, they talked without stopping. Or rather, the women talked. They did not seem to be conducting conversations; it was more a case of the women talking *at* their husbands. In a tone of slight annoyance, which did not seem to bother the men. Now and then, I suppose when some kind of reply couldn't be avoided, they growled something or other, but most of the time they kept quiet. Anyway, on the flight I thought how nice they were, those gnarled old married couples. How good it was that they stuck to their opinions, making a fuss, being difficult, instead of being just a docile crowd. At the same time, of course, it was a great strain to spend a long flight sitting beside one of these couples. Every ten minutes, and I'm hardly exaggerating, I had to stand up, since I was in the aisle seat, because the wife wanted to stretch her legs, go up to the front of the plane, talk to some of her acquaintances, or because she thought her husband ought to go to the toilet. At first she excused herself, and I said, 'No problem,' but after a while we stopped doing that. She would nudge me, I would stand up for her, and as we were about to land I had the feeling that we had become friends.

That reminded me very much of my grandparents. I could easily imagine them on a flight like this. In the window seat my grandfather, probably wanting to read, but prevented from doing so by my grandmother's remarks. She would have objected to the cramped seats, she'd have said the pilot had a nice voice, she would have commented unfavourably on the stewardesses' short skirts. And probably she would have talked to them at as much length as the woman next to me on the Israel Airlines flight, asking if it really wasn't possible to pay a quick visit to the toilet when the red lights had only just gone on? Or at least have another coffee? Turbulence? Oh, that made no difference. She'd be able to hold a cup of coffee. It was against the regulations? Never mind that, a coffee, please. You too, Pista? Two coffees, then.

Is that typically Jewish? That eternal discussion, something I'm inclined to indulge in myself, to the annoyance of people whom I contradict just to see how far I can get. Typically Jewish: does such a frame of mind exist?

My Jewish friends—and I do have some—say it does. They say, you don't like the world of nature, you prefer cities?

Typically Jewish. You can always come up with an 'On the other hand'? Typical. You have fads about food, you hate travelling, you would like to have the same moderate continental weather every day of the year? Typical. However, I suspect my Jewish friends also think it typically Jewish, in some circumstances, to stir a lot of hot wasabi into your soy sauce, to be allergic to Vitamin C, to dislike horseback riding. And maybe it's typically Jewish to think everything is typically Jewish.

Is it typically Jewish to kill yourself when you have survived the Holocaust—so then you determine for yourself how you want to die? Many concentration camp survivors did commit suicide later. Primo Levi is only the most famous. Another who did it—he survived the war in England—was the Hungarian journalist and writer Arthur Koestler. My grandmother liked his books very much. He and his wife, a married couple of Hungarian Jews, took their own lives in 1983.

Or is it typically Hungarian?

Hungary has one of the highest suicide rates in the world. Is there something like a Hungarian soul that does not set much store by life? Is it just coincidence that it was a Hungarian, Reszö Seress, who in 1933 wrote a song so hopelessly sad that it set off a wave of suicides? It's said that over a hundred people all over Europe took their own lives to the sounds of his tune, 'Gloomy Sunday'. The words ran: 'On my last Sunday, beloved, oh come to me.' The composer jumped from the roof of his house to his own death in 1968.

However, it must also be said that most Hungarians do not kill themselves.

‡

The sky above Copenhagen is a radiant cobalt blue, the leaves on the trees glow in all shades of red and yellow. It is so warm in the sun that even a fly has woken up, having made its way inside the car that my grandfather is just taking out of the garage, a brown Toyota with pale leather upholstery, and now it is buzzing against the window desperately trying to find a way out. My grandmother is sitting in the passenger seat with the dog on its leash at her feet. She is wearing a Loden coat that she bought years ago in a shop in Munich selling traditional Bavarian clothing; it is black wool with red back-stitching, and she has on her usual sturdy, pale shoes and a silk scarf. A small packet lies on the shelf in front of her, and the dog's basket is on the back seat.

My grandfather has dressed, and is now wearing a coarse tweed suit that has become much too large for him in these last few months—his throat, emerging from it, looks very thin. He has on the perforated leather gloves without fingertips that he always wears for driving. Because my grandmother thought it was chilly he has tucked a cravat into the collar of his shirt. He sits so upright on the driver's seat that his upper back does not touch the seat. The sun is low in the sky.

'Mucika, do you have my sunglasses there?'

My grandmother searches the glove compartment and brings out a pair of clip-on dark lenses that she fits over his glasses.

'Are you sure it's a good idea for you to drive?'

'Yes.'

'I don't think it is.'

'I'm fine.'

'Very well. As you like.'

My grandmother looks out the window, offended. At her feet, the dog begins panting. She always gets completely out of breath during a drive, evidently under the impression that she is covering the distance on foot as the surroundings outside the window move past. It is impossible to take her on long journeys; a drive on the autobahn once almost killed her, but my grandparents like taking Mitzi with them on small errands in the car.

I always felt ill in any car driven by my grandfather. At the wheel he revealed a part of his nature that was otherwise completely absent. He drove very aggressively, ignoring the regulations for giving way and other rules of the road, and from one moment to the next could be overcome by a fit of rage and curse the driver of the car in front of him. What's more, the car always stank of cigar smoke. That day, however, he drives at a moderate pace. And apart from theirs, there is hardly a car on the roads.

Small, detached bungalows pass by to the left and right of them. The front gardens are well-tended, the pavements are clean. Twice a week the city roads department collects the leaves that the residents have swept into tidy heaps. At almost every garden gate a notice warns you of the dog. A few weeks ago a fox was spotted in this area; it must have lost its way in the nearby forest and ended up here. Since then some of the smaller dogs are not allowed out of the house during the day, and it is noticeably quieter in this neighbourhood than usual.

They are approaching the first major road junction.

'Mucika, which way do I go here?'

'You'll send me out of my mind. You go this way every day. You turn off here. Here, Pista, on the right.'

My grandfather did indeed drive this way almost daily. On his own he can find his way perfectly well, but once my grandmother is with him he feels uncertain. Or let's say he feels it's safer to be uncertain. For many years he has been asking my grandmother which way to go at this point, and for many years my grandmother has been telling him to turn right here. Those are the roles they play. He asks in a pleasant tone, she turns her eyes to heaven and answers in annoyance. To other people, their dialogue sounds like a quarrel. But they are not quarrelling, they are simply speaking their lines.

My grandfather flicks on the indicator, looks in the rear-view mirror to be on the safe side, although there is not a vehicle to be seen far and wide except for theirs, and then turns right. They are now driving down a small street. My grandmother switches on the radio and searches for a station broadcasting classical music, but all she can find is pop. She switches off again.

'Watch out!' says my grandmother suddenly.

My grandfather very nearly fails to see a cyclist, who is now visible in the rear-view mirror gesticulating furiously.

'Please do concentrate, Pista,' says my grandmother angrily—whether she is angry with her husband or the cyclist, she herself doesn't know.

'Do you have my cigarillos?' asks my grandfather, who is a little shaken himself. Perhaps he really would have done better to stay at home.

My grandmother takes a pack out of her bag, lights one, and gives it to him.

'Thank you.'

She lights herself a cigarette. Neither says anything until they have passed a few road junctions. There is nothing to be heard but the car engine, the dog's shallow panting, and the slight hiss of the cigarette burning every time she draws on it.

'There. Stop there,' says my grandmother, pointing to a letterbox. 'Please, Pista, stop,' she repeats, although my grandfather is already braking.

'Shall I park the car?' he asks.

'No, just switch on the warning lights.'

He stops on the right of the road, pulls the handbrake on and switches on the warning lights, leaving the engine running. My grandmother takes the packet that was lying on the shelf, gives the dog's leash to my grandfather, and gets out of the car. My grandfather closes his eyes for a moment. This is the first time he has been out for days; it is a great strain on him. When my grandmother opens the car door again, he is startled, clears his throat and tries to look alert.

'Did you send Erzsi my best wishes?' he asks.

'Warning lights,' says my grandmother.

My grandfather switches off the warning lights.

'I even signed your name to the letter,' says my grandmother.

'Ah,' says my grandfather. He says it appreciatively, as if whistling through his teeth.

The fly is suddenly heard buzzing again, although much more quietly than before. It has probably strayed into the back of the car.

My grandfather stops outside a yellow house. He switches the engine off. The dog, panting heavily now, gets up on her hind legs, looks out the window, and wags her tail faster and faster. My grandmother puts on a pair of sunglasses. Her eyes are invisible behind the large, dark lenses.

'You must say goodbye to each other now,' says my grandmother.

She pulls the dog away from the window and pushes her in the direction of my grandfather, who takes the dog's head in both hands and tugs her whiskers lovingly. The dog accepts this, as she accepts everything, with her ears laid back and an unhappy expression.

'Szerbusz, Mitzike,' says my grandfather. 'Szerbusz. Jó édes Mitzike, jó kis kutya.' The last syllable comes out of his mouth as a high squeak, which he himself dislikes so much that he says no more. He leans over to the dog and gives her a kiss on the nose, which is cool and damp. Then he strokes her head a few times, so hard that she has to brace herself not to fall over. After that he pats her three times firmly on the back, and looks at my grandmother, who is breathing as heavily as if she had been holding her breath for minutes on end. She straightens up and puts her shoulders back. 'Gyere Mitzi, come along.'

She opens the car door, and the dog jumps out at once. The sound of barking is heard from the yellow house. My grandmother gets out of the car, forced to move faster than she likes because of the way the dog is tugging at her leash. 'Just a moment,' she says. 'The basket.' She opens the back door of the car and takes the basket off the seat. The dog is now excited, she is tugging her towards the garden gate and wagging her tail harder than ever. The door of the yellow house opens, and a dog that looks just like Mitzi, only rather taller and slimmer, races to the garden gate, followed by a tall blonde woman of around fifty. My grandfather closes his eyes.

‡

On an early autumn morning, I am sitting in the dining room of the same yellow house in Copenhagen, and the table in front of me is laid for coffee and cakes. An old man sits opposite me, and neither of us knows what to say to the other, or in what language, so we just smile across the table now and then, both of us probably hoping that his wife will be back soon. We are only a few streets away from the house where my grandparents lived. I have forgotten to ask the man's name, but his wife is called Inga. She is the woman who took charge of the dog back then. In four years' time the tall blonde woman, just over fifty when they left the dog with her, will be seventy years old.

Inga comes into the dining room with a tray of coffee and apple cake, and turns on the light, a Danish designer lamp which is the only modern item in the room. The apples are from their own garden, she says, putting large portions on our plates. We eat a few mouthfuls, saying 'Mmm,' and smiling. How do I broach the subject of my grandparents' double suicide? I begin with the dog. I tell Inga that Mitzi lived with us in Munich for a few years longer, getting more and more neurotic and anxious, and finally died a natural death of old age. We all learnt Hungarian for the sake of the dog, but even so she never fitted in. Yes, Mitzi was a remarkable dog, says Inga, nodding, and we are back in the past.

My grandmother had called the day before, says Inga. To ask if she could look after Mitzi for a few days, something they always did for each other when they went away. Yes, of course, Inga had said, but she couldn't take the dog before Sunday because she was busy until then. So they had agreed that my grandmother would bring her along on Sunday. Inga says my grandmother said they were going to Munich. She had said several times in the last few months that she and Pista were planning to spend the last years of their lives there, and now they were going to look at a few possible apartments.

Munich?

That was what my grandmother had told her, says Inga.

Without asking if I would like it, she puts a second slice of cake on my plate.

What had my grandmother been like that day?

She had seemed a little abstracted, quieter than usual, says Inga, perhaps a little sad. She had explained that to herself by thinking that it couldn't be easy for someone of Vera's age to move again. With her life story. Another new country.

Did she know my grandmother as a happy woman?

'Oh, yes,' says Inga. 'She was a very happy person. Always good-tempered. She lived for her husband.'

Inga and my grandmother had made friends through their dogs. They had fallen into conversation one day in the forest because they had the only two Irish terriers in Charlottenlund, and from then on they used to go walking their dogs together. If they did the full circuit it took them a good hour, if they cut it short they were out for forty minutes.

Did my grandmother tell her much about herself?

Inga thinks. 'No, not really. She was a very private person. She didn't give away any personal details.'

What did they talk about?

'Music. Opera, concerts. The ballet.'

I wonder how often my grandmother went to concerts. And what kind of concerts? Top international orchestras, or organ recitals in the Town Hall?

Did my grandmother ever talk about the old days in Hungary?

'No. No. Oh yes, wait, she did talk about her father.'

What did she say?

'She said he was in the navy. I remember that very well because I thought it was so funny. A naval officer—well, I'm sure you can see how odd that is!'

Her husband, who has been sitting there in silence all this time, nods.

'I mean, what's a Hungarian doing in the navy?' says Inga, looking amused. 'Hungary doesn't even have a sea-coast.'

I say that as far as I know he was an engineer. Inga shook her head, no, no, he went to sea. She laughs. I suspect that my grandmother may have thought this version up because she liked it better. Or perhaps he really had been a naval officer in the First World War? And doesn't the navy need engineers? However, who knows how it really was!

I ask how she would describe her relationship with my grandmother.

'I thought she was fascinating,' says Inga. 'She always wore trousers. She was a good friend, older than me, and I admired her.'

As I am leaving I think that my grandmother must have been very fond of Inga. She needed such people. She needed them the way an actress needs an audience. They were friends, but they didn't really know each other. My grandmother's real friends, it suddenly occurs to me, were all Jews.

‡

Did you ever have a Jewish boyfriend? A friend of mine asked me that one day over lunch. She is Jewish, and she lives in New York. I acted as if I had to think for a moment, which in fact I didn't, and said no. She thought that was funny. Perhaps I was missing something, perhaps there was a tacit understanding that it couldn't work with a non-Jew? The question was probably also for herself, as her husband isn't Jewish, and theirs is a very happy marriage. Had I ever heard of J-Date, she asked. No, I hadn't. She explained that J-Date was an online dating portal for Jews. Ah, I said, and I was about to change the subject when she suddenly brought her son into the conversation, a successful doctor who met his future wife, who'd have thought it, through J-Date. Yes, but I don't want to try online dating, I protested. It was no use, she simply refused to talk about anything else, and after she had spent about an hour and a half explaining the many advantages of this way of making contacts, saying repeatedly that I had nothing to lose, I gave in: J-Date, I agreed, was just what I needed. I would sign on today. I would get to meet a great many interesting New Yorkers, all of them Jewish, and they might even be nice as well. What more could I ask for?

Back in the apartment in Brooklyn where I was living for a few months, I turned on the computer at once, went to the J-Date internet site—and signed on. I called myself Johannaberlin, from which you can perhaps gather that I really hadn't wasted much time thinking about it, no, I wanted to know now, at once. I wasn't going to be in New York for very long, so I had no time to lose. I wrote my profile as honestly as I could: I had a Hungarian father of Jewish origin and a German mother, I said, and when I was in Tel Aviv recently it had felt, to my own surprise, as if I were coming home, so I could imagine that a Jewish boyfriend might not be such a bad idea. 'I don't know,' I wrote, 'because I've never had one. My grandparents were Holocaust survivors, and they never talked about their Jewish identity, any more than my father does. So that part of myself is almost unknown to me.' And then I added that I liked spring better than autumn, winter better than summer, that I like reading, I have some great friends, and on a plane I always like to have an aisle seat. The kind of thing you write when you want to be thought pleasant to meet, without knowing by whom.

Within a few days I had 130 messages, from 130 men wanting to meet me, introducing themselves and their hobbies, men who were doctors, architects, lawyers, fitness trainers, actors, or journalists. And every one of them was Jewish. I was overwhelmed.

At first I read everything. Their entire profiles, including favourite foods, favourite sporting activities, notions about the ideal partnership. After a few days of this I could tell, after two or three practised glances, whether someone was just like most of the others ('I love nature, I enjoy sports and I have many interests'). I preferred those who sounded more original; there were about eight of them. Eight out of 130. I whittled the number down to five, and finally met two of them. After all, for someone who had never in her life liked the idea of online dating, that was a surprisingly high number.

The first was called Victor. He had attracted my interest with an astute analysis of my thoughts about the seasons. 'So you like winter because spring follows it, and you like spring because summer comes next. So the season you really prefer is summer.'

I met him at a café. Or rather I almost didn't meet him, because as I learned on this first internet date of my life, if someone tells you in his profile that he is thirty-six years old, it doesn't necessarily mean that he is thirty-six. It can mean that one or two decades ago he *was* thirty-six, and still has a lively memory of what it felt like. And if someone describes his figure in his profile as 'athletic', it doesn't necessarily mean that he really has an athletic figure. Far from it. And if he describes his place of origin as 'some neighbourhood', then you should remember that this neighbourhood may turn out to have been in St Petersburg.

You can imagine what a surprise it was, then, to see not a thirty-six-year-old, brown-haired, athletic American but an elderly, stocky man with a grey beard come over to my table and ask, in a Russian accent, 'Are you Johannaberlin?'

When I asked him, a little later, why he hadn't said in his profile that he came from Russia, he smiled, waggled his head, and said, 'I dropped a hint. I wrote that I speak English and Russian.' So much for Victor.

Sasha, on the other hand, really did look as nice as his photograph. He was also the age he had said he was, and it was even true that he was a journalist. The fact that nothing came of it was for reasons that can't be resolved in advance.

‡

It is very quiet when my grandparents get back to their house. No dog jumping happily up at the door on the inside when the key is turned in the lock, no paws pattering over the wooden floor to welcome them. An empty house. But it still smells of dog.

My grandmother hangs her coat on the coat-stand, my grandfather changes from his outdoor shoes to his slippers, which takes him some time. He supports himself on the door frame, first treading down the back of his left shoe with the toe of his right shoe, and slipping it off, then taking the right shoe off with the toes of his left foot. My grandmother watches him.

'Wouldn't you like to lie down, Pista?'

'There's no need.'

'Aren't you tired? You look tired.'

'Well, yes, I'm a little tired. But shouldn't I stay awake?'

'What for?'

'To give you a hand.'

'What with?'

'Well, what are you going to do now?'

'You'll send me out of my mind yet. I told you just now in the car. I'm going into the garden, and later I'll be packing up presents. Really, Pista, you can go and lie down. I'll be fine without your help.'

'Very well. I'll sit on the sofa.'

'Good. You do that.'

My grandfather goes slowly into the living room. My grandmother glances at her little gold watch. Two in the afternoon. She locks the front door from the inside with the key. Then she takes the key out of the lock and puts it on the chest of drawers.

‡

It occurs to me that I have forgotten to ask Hélène where my grandparents stayed when they were in Paris. Did they have

an apartment of their own? Where, in which arrondissement? Or did they stay at a hotel? I could call her; if Hélène
remembers the answer, it is only a phone number away. But I
don't make the call. I am afraid of seeming too demanding.
During my research I often feel afraid that I am being a
nuisance. I feel like an intruder, a thief trying to take something from the people who have agreed to talk to me about
my grandparents. Almost every time I ask a question I feel
discourteously inquisitive. As if I were sticking my nose into
what's none of my business. Why should I want to know how
my grandparents spent their lives? Who am I to try finding
out things that they didn't talk about, some of them perhaps
very private? I asked Erzsi whether my grandparents were
faithful to each other. At first she hesitated, then she said that
as far as she knew each had been unfaithful to the other
once, but that had been back in Hungary, and she didn't
know the details. I could tell, even as she spoke, that she was
regretting having answered my question at all. And then I too
felt it had been very indiscreet of me, and I quickly changed
the subject.

It was much the same with my aunt, whom I visited in
Copenhagen several times in the course of my research. At
first I just asked away, asked about everything I wanted to
know. Then, after a while, I sensed some resistance. I realised
that she didn't want to talk so much about her parents, and

that she couldn't discuss them as if they were simply a fascinating couple. They were her mother and father. Her parents who had killed themselves. Difficult parents, too. So a time came when I stopped asking my aunt about my grandparents. But I paid attention to every casual mention she made of them, and then, feeling as if I were acting surreptitiously, wrote it down in a notebook. I wonder how I would like it if someone were writing a book about my own parents. What would I talk about? Only the good parts? Would I want anyone to write about them at all? Probably not, I think. I would be afraid that the researcher's picture of them would not coincide with mine.

So I don't phone Hélène again. What does it matter where my grandparents stayed in Paris?

‡

In May 1991, five months before the death of my grandparents, my brother and his current girlfriend visited them in Copenhagen. He saw them only for one evening, because next morning my grandparents were going to Hungary, and my brother and his girlfriend were to look after their house for a week. My brother says that his girlfriend thought our grandparents were very interesting. He tells me that when she and my brother were alone together for a moment, she asked him about the story of their lives. They were Jewish, how had they survived the war? And since my brother didn't really know the answer to that, he decided he would simply ask my grandfather about it directly—and he did, too, with his girlfriend present.

What was it really like in the concentration camp?

He didn't want to talk about it, replied my grandfather, as might have been expected. There was a pause, in which my brother tried to think of some neutral subject to which he could turn instead. Then my grandfather suddenly said that there was another of his experiences he could talk about. And he told my brother about the Korean War.

He spent seven months in Korea in 1952, working as a reconstructive surgeon. He had seen some terrible things, he told my brother. He had had to stitch many arms and legs back into place. And with that my brother's memory comes to an end, either because my grandfather said no more, or because this was another subject that he didn't want to talk about—and memory is sometimes courteous enough to delete such matters at once out of consideration.

What was my grandfather doing in the Korean War? What was a Hungarian doing there at all? And furthermore a Hungarian who had survived a war only through luck just a few years earlier?

I find a Hungarian journalist who spent several months in North Korea in 1952 and 1953, reporting on the war for the press at home. In his reports, which can be accessed through the British Library, I read about a hospital donated by Hungary to its fellow-socialist country North Korea, a whole hospital, complete with doctors, nurses and medical equipment. It was in a small village called Chung-wha, about thirty kilometres from the capital Pyongyang, and it was housed in a former school building which was in a very primitive condition. A large Red Cross was painted on the roof, in the hope that the American enemy would refrain from bombing it.

The journalist now lives in Paris. On the phone, he tells me that some twelve Hungarian doctors worked there, although he did not know them all by name. One of them must have been my grandfather, he says, because no Hungarian doctors took part in the Korean War anywhere else. Were they made to go, I ask him, or did they volunteer? And I tell him a little of my grandfather's story. Going to Korea was good for your career, he says. Especially for Jewish doctors. Or put it the other way around: not taking part in this mission would have given a negative impression.

The Hungarian doctors, he says, worked day and night. They saved the lives of people who had been burnt almost to death by napalm bombing, including many women and children from the rural population. At night, when the Americans carried out their heaviest air raids, they operated in a cellar without windows, so that no light could be seen from outside. They had been treating their patients in conditions of deadly danger, says the journalist. They worked miracles.

‡

In the summer of 1952, when my grandfather was in Korea, my grandmother took the children to the bathing resort of Csillaghegy. Erzsi visited her there. She had never seen my grandmother in such a bad state before, she tells me. Vera had been sick with worry. Tense and unfriendly. Her behaviour had been impossible. She scarcely even said hello, although Erzsi had come out into the country by train to see her. Erzsi makes a face clearly typical of my grandmother: chin up, eyebrows raised, nostrils slightly dilated. Erzsi says she went around on tiptoe so as not to make matters even worse; she tried to be particularly friendly, if not invisible. But it was no use. My grandmother had been gloomy and taciturn all day, giving Erzsi the feeling that she was to blame for something.

When Erzsi tells me about this she does it in dramatic form, taking different parts.

Erzsi: 'What's the matter with you?'

Erzsi as my grandmother: 'Nothing. Nothing at all.'

'Of course there's something the matter. Come on, tell me.'

Finally my grandmother shouted at her, 'Go away, go away, get out of here.'

Erzsi: 'That's no way to speak to me.'

At that, she says, my grandmother burst into tears. 'Nobody loves me,' she said, and she cried her eyes out.

Erzsi: 'Yes, they do, Veruska. You're my best friend. It's all right.'

'No. Nobody loves me.'

And then, says Erzsi, after a while they sat down and talked. And my grandmother told her that she was sick with worry in case something might happen to my grandfather in Korea, she couldn't sleep or eat. She was going to kill herself, she said, if he didn't come back.

It was the second time she had said that.

‡

The sun has disappeared behind the blue spruce trees that grow at the end of my grandparents' garden, it is noticeably colder now than only a few days ago, a damp chill rises from the lawn. My grandmother has put a cardigan round her shoulders. She stands at the far end of the terrace, looking at her garden, which she regards as her creation. Almost every day she pulls out weeds somewhere, straightens a clematis tendril that has been caught on something on its way upwards, prunes branches, rakes up leaves, or tells my grandfather that the grass needs mowing, a job that he then does with appropriate care and the electric lawnmower.

Her greatest love is for her roses, which form a natural rose hedge between the terrace and the lawn—white 'Iceberg', pale pink cottage roses, yellow 'Golden Border', crimson 'Prince', violet 'Chartreuse de Parme'—their names are noted on plant labels stuck in the ground. Over the years she has become an expert, she knows that 'Ophelia' is a good climber, 'American Beauty' does not like too much sun, she knows when purple 'Marbrée' will flower for the second time. Of course she also has 'Queen of Denmark', a particularly hardy rose and easy to grow, with pale pink flowers and small, bluish, soft thorns.

And the roses never flower more beautifully than at this time of year. It is as if the flowers are offering up all they can give before winter comes. They seem to glow, their colours are so bright, and the scent is more intense than in spring or summer. My grandmother smells a yellow rose that is just about to fade. The word 'beguiling' comes into her mind. She once read somewhere that roses do better if you talk to them, and since then she has done that, she talks to them as if they were friends to be greeted and complimented on their looks. Oh, how beautiful you are, she tells a particularly multi-petalled 'Versigny' that resembles a pale pink cabbage lettuce—de szép lettél, she speaks

Hungarian to her roses. Then she goes into the little tool shed to find some compost, because although it is still rather too early she is going to get the roses ready to survive the winter.

As she walks across the terrace she hears music coming from the house, and stops. Schumann's piano concerto, she loves it. She goes to the living room window to tell my grandfather to turn it up louder. Or open the window.

Through the pane, she sees him sitting on the sofa. She taps. He doesn't seem to hear her. He looks as if he is concentrating hard. She taps again, louder. He doesn't react. He is sitting on the sofa and does not look up. She taps and calls his name. Still no reaction. It suddenly strikes her how thin he is. His head looks far too large on his narrow shoulders, he seems almost like a child. A child grown old, thin, with sunken cheeks, a white moustache and glasses. It saddens her to see him like that. It also moves her. This is the man with whom she has grown old. Her husband. Her life.

‡

On the afternoon of 23 October 1956 my father and my aunt, twelve and nine years old at the time, stand behind the bars over the living room window on the second floor, looking down at the Oktogon. The gigantic statue of Stalin that until a few moments ago stood on its plinth in Heroes' Square is being dragged along, accompanied by thousands of demonstrators. My father still remembers what a loud noise Stalin made as he was hauled over the asphalt.

A few hours later they heard shots fired. The demonstration that had begun peacefully, Hungarian independence from the Soviet Union being its principal demand, had become a bloody revolution. Shots were exchanged between the demonstrators and the police in the square in front of the radio building; that evening some 200,000 people assembled outside Parliament demanded the re-appointment of the reforming communist Imre Nagy as head of government. He was in fact then appointed head of state, and after four days of bloody fighting the first Russian troops left the country. It looked as if liberty had triumphed: Hungary seceded from the Warsaw Pact and declared its neutrality. The crisis seemed to be over.

But it all turned out differently. On 29 October Israel attacked Egypt, which Britain and France, in their own turn, took as the occasion for an attack on the Suez Canal. For a moment the attention of the world was diverted from events in Eastern Europe. The Soviet Union took its chance. On 4 November thousands of Russian tanks crossed the city border of Budapest, and there was heavy fighting. There were 2500 dead on the Hungarian side in the days to come, on the Soviet side a little over 700. This is a conservative estimate.

Revolutionaries hid in the Orthopaedic Hospital where my grandfather was director. He knew they were there; he was offering his own passive resistance to the Soviet occupying force. Was he aware of the danger to which he was thereby exposing himself—and his family? Probably. The idea of flight was raised.

My father was just twelve at the time. How much did he understand of all this?

He still remembers that they kept listening to the radio news at home, and as soon as he and his little sister came into the room voices dropped to a whisper. He and his cousin were told about the plans for flight; I suppose my grandparents had decided that the two boys were old enough not to give the game away. One day, he says, they went to the hospital. They slept there for a few nights. Then he and his mother went back to the apartment on the Oktogon once more to fetch a few things. They packed a bag with what they could take, and went back to the hospital with it; to get there they must have crossed one of the bridges over the Danube. And a day later, or perhaps the same day, he doesn't remember which, they fled. Which means only that they got into the black DKW outside the Orthopaedic Hospital in Buda, and drove towards the border. All flights have to begin somehow.

‡

My aunt, who lives in Copenhagen, has to fetch a step-ladder from her lumber room to get to the very top of her wardrobe, right at the back of the shelf, to reach the bag which my father and my grandmother had brought back from the apartment. It was the only thing they took with them on their flight from Hungary. A well-preserved reddish-brown travelling bag with handles, slightly smaller than a small trunk. If you open the zip, the smell of the air in my grandparents' house rises to your nostrils even today.

They fled on 20 November 1956. My aunt says no one told her about the forthcoming flight. She was nine years old, so perhaps they were afraid of alarming her. Or they thought she might tell other people, and then they would all be in danger. Whenever she entered a room the conversation died away, she does remember that. And then she was suddenly told one afternoon: come along, we're going to stay at the hospital where your father works for a couple of days. And a little while after that they said, come along, now we're going to get in the car and drive away. No one told her where they were going. No one explained that they would not be coming back. There it was again, the typical we-don't-talk-about-that attitude.

My aunt thought the atmosphere in the car was threatening. My father and her cousin István sat beside her, two boys who were normally always annoying her, winding her up, pestering her, and now for a change they kept perfectly quiet. My grandfather drove, my grandmother sat in the front passenger seat. She told my aunt that if they were stopped she must pretend to be asleep. One can imagine more reassuring situations for a nine-year-old.

My father remembers that it was light when they set out and dark when they reached the border. He says they had been driving for about three hours. They were stopped just before the border. They had to get out. A Hungarian border guard bent down to my father and asked if he was cold. My father nodded. The soldier took off his right glove and gave it to my father. He still has it: a brown leather glove with only two fingers, for the thumb and the forefinger. Those are all you need to fire a gun.

They had to leave their car behind, and then they were allowed to go on.

My father remembers walking over an open field. It was cold, the moon was shining, no one said a word. Suddenly there were people behind them, and as they didn't know who the people were and whether they were well-disposed or not, they ducked down in alarm behind a bale of straw and waited. After a while, when nothing had happened for some time, they went on again. Soon they saw the lights of houses, and a church tower, they went faster, heard voices that were not speaking Hungarian, saw street signs in

German in the darkness—and realised that they were on Austrian soil.

‡

Erzsi fled two nights after my grandparents. She was unlucky; it rained that night. She was wearing a fur coat that my grandmother had given her a few days earlier as a goodbye present, and because she herself couldn't take it with her. Erzsi and her three small children fled on foot. Their flight was unplanned, and had to be undertaken suddenly and in great haste, as her husband had been arrested, and she was trying to get herself and the children to safety. Erzsi was wearing the fur coat, and it was raining, and all she could think was: I hope the rain doesn't ruin the fur, I'm sure Vera would be cross if she knew. Because Erzsi's husband was considered an enemy of the state she did not go over the border at a guarded crossing point, but climbed a barbed wire fence in the dark. Erzsi got the coat stuck on the barbed wire, tore a hole in it, and then stumbled into a furrow in a field that of course was muddy from the rain. Flight was one thing—whining children, cold, wet, and the thought of her husband in prison—the coat was another. Erzsi was determined to give it back to my grandmother. She knew her well enough to be sure that my grandmother was secretly counting on that if they ever met again. All through her flight she thought of nothing but the fur coat, cursing the rain, the mud and the barbed wire. And when they really did see each other again in Vienna, when they met there by chance among thousands of refugees, Erzsi gave my grandmother back her goodbye present of the fur coat, and my grandmother accepted it—graciously, we may assume. It was 'in poor condition', says Erzsi. She still seems to feel bad about that.

‡

In the first photographs showing my grandparents in their new country of Denmark, they look frozen. They are lying on deckchairs outside a wooden house, wearing thick coats and scarves, with rugs over them, blinking at the northern sun. They cycle along gravel paths, my grandmother and my aunt wearing headscarves, and with their dark eyebrows they look more Hungarian in this flat landscape than ever before. The Lippmann family had arranged for them to stay in the summer house of some acquaintances of theirs in Rungsted, a little seaside town. Many Danes took in refugees from Hungary with great warmth and kindness.

They had arrived in Denmark on a Saturday, and on the following Monday my father, my aunt and her cousin started school, without understanding a word of Danish. They picked it up at different speeds. My father says that one morning in March, just a few months after they had come to Denmark, he realised that he could understand the news on the radio. It took my aunt longer. For the first few months she didn't say a word, and then one day she opened her mouth and spoke Danish perfectly, without any mistakes and with no accent. My grandparents were never to lose their heavy Hungarian accent entirely. Their Danish always sounded dark and lilting, instead of scratchy and high up in the throat, although that was not necessarily a disadvantage.

My grandfather began working after only a few weeks, first in a hospital in Kolding, soon, once he became known in Denmark as an orthopaedic surgeon, in the Orthopaedic Hospital in Copenhagen. At first he could hardly communicate at all verbally, but ganglions are international, after all. And my grandmother went to great pains to be a Danish housewife. She almost overdid it. If there was ever a perfect example of a proper Danish woman, she personified it. She made friends with women in the neighbourhood, learned to sew, took up gardening—which had never interested her in Budapest, perhaps for lack of a garden. She got a dog, an Irish terrier called Paidi, whom I even knew myself when he was blind and frail in his old age. She managed money even better than she used to in Hungary. And she learned to cook and bake. She had never done that in Budapest either, and why would she when they had a cook?

They had shed their old life as you get rid of a jacket when you have tired of it. What mattered now was their new life in Denmark. In order to learn the language, my grandmother translated Hungarian recipes into Danish—where she got the recipes in the first place no one knows—and in the end she even published her best recipes for goulash, dumplings, yeast braids and letscho as a cookery book. On the title page she is smiling at the camera, placing a steaming bowl on a Danish teak table. She looks so demure in that picture, serving a meal with her apron on and such a friendly expression on her face, that I can't help thinking of the story of The Wolf and the Seven Little Kids, in which the wolf ate chalk to sweeten his voice.

They bought new furniture and a car, they went to concerts, they invited new friends to meals, they enjoyed walking beside something as exotic as the sea. In all, their immigration can be considered a complete success. My grandfather became a successful surgeon, they paid their taxes reluctantly but on the dot, like all good citizens, and they ate *frokost* in the morning. At Christmas, which they called Jul in Danish, they followed the Scandinavian custom of dancing hand in hand around the tree with their children and later their grandchildren. They even liked King Frederick IX, and after him his daughter Queen Margrethe, the latter perhaps not least because she, too, is a chain smoker.

‡

My grandfather is sitting in the living room on the deep, red sofa where my grandparents always watched TV in the evenings. They liked American crime series such as 'Columbo' best, but they also enjoyed the German series 'Derrick', shown on Danish TV in the original with subtitles. Now, however, the TV set is switched off. My grandfather has a rug over his legs and a small pair of nail scissors in his hand, and he is busy cutting open capsules full of white powder. He tips the contents alternately into first one and then the other of two glasses standing on the coffee table in front of him. The third movement of Schumann's piano concerto in A minor is coming over the loudspeakers, the *allegro vivace*, Martha Argerich with the National Symphony Orchestra conducted by Mstislav Rostropovich. Capsule by capsule the level of powder in the glasses rises; he has already cut a great many capsules open, and the empty cases lie on the table in front of him. If he looked up he could see my grandmother coming over the terrace with a large bunch of freshly cut roses. She walks quickly, stooping slightly forward, the sun will soon set, it is chilly outside now.

By this time he has worked out the ideal method of opening the capsules. First he jabs the point of the scissors into the middle of a capsule, then he enlarges the hole by boring through it with the blades and shaking the capsule slightly to right and left. Then he takes out the blades, places them neatly at the centre and, making small surgical incisions, he cuts once around the capsule.

Out of the corner of his eye he sees my grandmother coming up to the window outside. He doesn't look up. He hears her call his name. He still doesn't look up.

And there's another capsule separated. He tips its contents into one of the glasses.

My grandmother taps the living-room window.

Not now, he thinks. There is something soothing about the work he is doing. Always the same, a hundred capsules, jab, cut, tip, a hundred times. He doesn't want to be disturbed just now. Not while he's distracting himself with this task.

She taps again.

My grandfather acts as if he hadn't heard it. He is trying to look totally absorbed in the work, in the music. He keeps his head bent and goes on working. Jab, cut, tip. Jab, cut, tip. Soon he really is absorbed in the job.

Next time he raises his head he sees my grandmother through the window back among the roses. She has a bag of garden compost in her hand. Good, thinks my grandfather, I'll be left in peace a little longer.

‡

A year after their arrival in Denmark my grandparents were interviewed by Danish Radio. Hungarian refugees—Denmark had taken in over a thousand—were something unusual in this small country, and people were interested to know how they were getting on. My father remembers that the radio interview sounded unintentionally funny. On this occasion my grandparents' usually deep voices had risen high with excitement, and by comparison with the radio reporter's voice sounded as if the recording had been speeded up. They had been given the questions in advance, because they were not entirely confident in their new language yet, so this way they could write their answers first and then read them out. My father still has the manuscript. It is typed, with much crossing out, and corrections in the margin in my grandmother's handwriting.

The first question is to my grandfather. He is asked about the leather bag hanging in the front hall. 'It's full of memories,' he replies. The memories are all they were able to take out of Hungary, because their decision to leave had been made almost on the spur of the moment. 'After the second Russian attack we were deeply depressed. We couldn't imagine ourselves going on living in a country governed by lies, a country that had disappointed us so much.'

'What was your flight like?' asks the Danish reporter.

'A little easier than we'd expected. We drove to the border, and although the border police gave us a fright at first, they even pointed out our way to Austria. They kept the car, but they let us go.'

'And why did you come to Denmark in particular?'

'It was chance,' says my grandfather, 'and I can say now that it was a very lucky chance.' And then he tells the reporter the story I have often heard myself, from my father, from my aunt—that during the revolution my grandfather had met a Dane who came to Budapest with aid deliveries from the Red Cross. When the situation worsened, the Dane was unable to leave the country, and by chance he found a place to stay in the hospital where my grandfather was in charge. His name was Ole Lippmann, and he was the first Dane my father had met in his life. He had been active in the Danish Resistance during the Second World War. My grandfather liked him, they made friends. And when my grandparents were wondering where to go—it was difficult, Vienna had proved cold and unfriendly, and none of the countries they had had in mind, Australia, Canada, America (the main thing being to get as far away from the Russians as possible!) was still taking refugees—they happened to pass the Danish Embassy. Why not Denmark? They went in, they had nothing to lose—and their names were already known to the Embassy, because Ole Lippmann had talked about them, and the Embassy people were expecting them to turn up. 'So Denmark became our future,' said my grandfather, thus consigning Hungary to the past.

Then the reporter turns to my grandmother.

'And what about you? How are you doing?'

'Very well now,' says my grandmother. 'But it was difficult at first. We'd had the wrong kind of upbringing in Hungary. It was a feudal system, and if you look at that system you shouldn't just think of its agriculture but the way it brings up young people. For instance, I never in all my life saw a man at work in the kitchen. When I saw a Danish man in the kitchen for the first time I thought it was his hobby. I was really surprised to find that he was a better cook than his wife. A household help is as common in Hungary as a whistling kettle in Denmark. We didn't have a washing machine, we had a washerwoman. If a young girl in Hungary gets a good education she sits her Year 12 exams. I had a good school education myself, but I'd never learnt to do the laundry and the ironing or the cooking.'

'And now you have?'

'Yes, but you can imagine what difficulties I had. One of the most difficult things is the way to iron a shirt, and I learnt that from a man.'

'Do you hope to go back to Hungary some day?'

'I did until not so long ago, but since last month I've really felt that we're at home in Denmark. If I go into town, or go shopping, I always have a picture of my home in my head. It used to be our apartment in Budapest that I saw— now I see our apartment in Hørsholm.'

Jews from Budapest had become Danish citizens. They didn't want to be conspicuous, they wanted to belong, no one was to know they had been communists, that they were Jewish, Jewish communists from Eastern Europe—none of that was to matter now. As Julika had said: life began in 1945. And another life now began in Denmark. My grandparents' third and last life.

Did they ever look back?

Once, doing something that must be described as extremely unusual for them, my grandparents visited the former concentration camp of Mauthausen together. This would have been in the late seventies or early eighties. They had just been to see us in Munich, they borrowed our Peugeot and drove there. When they came back in the afternoon, all my grandfather said was: 'Going there by car is much nicer than going on foot.'

‡

'Look.' My grandmother comes into the living room. My grandfather looks up. She is carrying a vase of long-stemmed, dark red roses, there must be thirty of them, the flowers almost fully open.

'Look,' she says again, holding the flowers to his nose. 'They're so fragrant.'

My grandfather smells them.

'Mmm,' he says. 'How beautiful they are. As beautiful as you.'

My grandfather has paid my grandmother so many compliments that by now she probably hardly notices them for what they are. After every invitation they accepted together when there were other women present, he would say, 'You were the most beautiful in the fish market.' ('Maga volt a legzebb a halpiacon.') Always the same wording, like the reassurances of the wicked stepmother's mirror in the fairy tale, she was the fairest of them all.

My grandmother puts the vase on the dining table. She adjusts a few petals until at last she is satisfied. Then she turns and stands there, undecided.

'Where did you put the book?' she asks my grandfather.

He has just been concentrating on tipping the contents of another opened capsule into one of the glasses. To get the last remnants out of it, he taps the halves of the capsule with his forefinger.

'The book,' says my grandmother impatiently. 'Pista, the book, where did you put it?'

My grandfather looks up. Ah yes, the book. He reaches between the cushions and brings it out. *Final Exit*, say the words on the cover. Above the title, smaller, in red lettering: 'The #1 New York Times Bestseller'.

‡

They had tried various ways of getting hold of this book, published in America in the spring of 1991. Almost unnoticed at first, the book became notorious after a long article in the *Wall Street Journal* in July. There had never before been a manual that anyone could buy on ways of committing suicide. That August *Final Exit* already headed the bestseller list of the *New York Times*, newspapers all over the world were discussing it, you could read about it even in Denmark. A book describing the most certain, cleanest, fastest way to take your own life. Exactly what my grandparents needed. My grandfather could operate on broken bones; he was not an anaesthetist. So how were they to come by *Final Exit*? The book was not sold in Denmark, or in Germany, or in any of the other countries of Europe except the Netherlands. But my grandparents didn't know anyone in the Netherlands, and the internet wasn't up and running yet.

First they tried a Danish doctor who was a friend of theirs. He did get hold of the book, he read it, and he decided not to pass it on to my grandparents. The methods set out in the book were so precise, so effective, that he felt he would be actively taking part in their plan if he was the one who gave them the book. He phoned my grandparents and said he was unwilling to help them. So my grandmother phoned Erzsi—after all, what was the use of a friend in America?

Erzsi says she didn't want to send my grandmother the book. But my grandmother was so pressing, and called so often, that in the end, she says, her husband bought the book and sent it to Copenhagen. Erzsi says my grandmother called again to say the package hadn't arrived. And that her husband finally bought another copy of the book and sent it to Copenhagen. The second copy did arrive.

‡

I order *Final Exit* from Amazon, and it comes by post two days later. A perfectly normal brown package. There is no disclaimer recommending you not to read the book if you are suffering from severe depression. Nor is there any sticker warning you that the contents are dangerous, not even a hopeful, 'Don't try this at home.' No, it's a perfectly normal paperback in English—no German translation has yet appeared—fitting comfortably in the hand, 156 pages, price 10.95 euros. I put it away at first and let it lie around the apartment unopened for a few days, front cover down. Now that I have a copy, it seems sinister to me.

When I first cautiously leaf through it, I begin by reading one of the methods of killing yourself described as particularly effective, which involves breathing in gas with a plastic bag over your head. I think at once of my grandfather. To have survived a concentration camp, and now this? I close the book again and put it in a cupboard, shutting both full-length doors. Although all my grandparents' feelings about that book had probably been positive—they'll have been relieved when it finally arrived in the post, they will have studied the details with curiosity—it seems to me as if the book killed them. As if it were a weapon that they had turned against themselves.

The time comes when I do read it after all. I begin with the foreword and end on the last page, it doesn't take long to read, and once you are through with the foreword, which sets out to justify the book and makes a plea for understanding, you can read it even faster. It is a practical guide to the best way of taking your own life, and it is meant for people who will have their own reasons for doing just that. In other words: this book will be very welcome to those who have already made up their minds to die. I am sure that *Final Exit* was a great help to my grandparents.

‡

At my parents' place in Munich, they have a bookshelf containing a few old photograph albums from the years 1956 to 1971. Most of the photos were taken by my father, and his initial enthusiasm for the technical potential of his camera is obvious: the album contains many artistic black and white pictures of tulips, the background sometimes clear-cut, sometimes blurred. There's even a series that must have been taken on Christmas Eve one year. Three people, presumably my grandparents and my aunt, are posing in front of what is presumably a tree, presumably decorated, and they may be waving at the camera; a few shadows in the upper part of the picture could be hands, but you can't be sure. The photographer was concentrating above all on getting the candle in the foreground in sharp focus.

In the 1956 album there is a loose picture, dated 12 December. It is on A4 paper, and on the back it is stamped 'Redaktion Aktuelt København', captioned 'Ungarske Flygtninge'. The photo shows my grandparents a month after their arrival in Denmark as 'Hungarian Refugees'; they look chic, as if nothing much had happened. My grandfather is wearing a beret and has a cigarillo between his lips. My grandmother wears a coat with a big fur collar and a finely striped silk scarf round her neck. Her hands are in black leather gloves. She has stuck a Danish newspaper casually under her arm. Any country would be glad to have refugees like them.

In the following years the family travelled Europe, as we can tell from black and white views of the Atomium in Brussels, of the Eiffel Tower and Sacré-Cœur, the arena in Verona, the Forum Romanum, and Piccadilly Circus. And again and again there are photographs of their new country:

the castle in Helsingör, the royal bodyguard, the Little Mermaid.

Summer 1964: a group photo of young flautists on a holiday course in Nice. My father is wearing dark horn-rimmed glasses, standing in the middle of the front row next to the flute teacher; on the right in the back row is a young woman with freckles, long dark hair and a fringe, my mother. That was the summer when they met.

Summer 1968: new house, new garden, new hobby— from now on all the pictures are in colour. My grandmother is playing croquet on a green lawn, wearing a pink and white check blouse and striking a silly pose for the camera.

August 1969: my aunt's wedding. In the photos of it in the album my grandmother is in the foreground. She wears a floor-length dark green dress, she has pinned her hair up on her head and wears a kind of diadem on it. She is beaming. Somewhere in the background my aunt is to be seen, wearing white. Erzsi has told me that my grandmother acted as if she were the bride. She reigned supreme at the wedding, along with my grandfather. Even at their own daughter's wedding. She and she alone was always the fairest of them all.

August 1971: my grandmother is holding her first grand-child in her arms, my cousin. He is only a few days old. She is laughing, she seems to like her new role. My grandfather is not in the picture. My aunt has told me how he reacted when she told him she was pregnant: 'You mean I'll soon be having to sleep with a grandmother?' She is only half smiling when she tells this story.

‡

In the year when I was born, 1971, a month after my cousin, my grandparents moved into the house in Charlottenlund where they were to spend the rest of their lives, and which lingers in my memory like no other house in the world, not even the houses where we ourselves lived. From here on I do not have to rely on other people's memory; I myself remember almost every detail. There was a chest of drawers here, a picture hung there—I stored it all inside me as if I had gone through the house with a camera at the time, making a film. Through the front door and straight ahead to the guestroom, zoom in on the picture on the wall there, a gloomy Chagall print of a man with a green face playing the violin, the camera travels back to the entrance hall and turns sharply right, where it passes through the large living room and goes into the kitchen.

It was a wooden house, built in a U-shape, a low-roofed bungalow painted brown, opening around a terrace at the back. As soon as you came in you were surrounded by that special smell, a mixture of my grandmother's perfume, plain soap, pumpernickel, damp wooden boards and dog, all enveloped in the obligatory cloud of cigarette smoke that never grew cold.

I particularly liked the skull that lay on the shelf in the entrance hall of my grandparents' house. It was real; it had been given to my father by a dentist who was a friend of his and who called it Maria, because apparently it came from the graveyard of a convent of nuns. There were still a few yellow teeth left in the jaws. My grandfather sometimes took it off the shelf for me, and then I held it reverently in my hand and shuddered pleasurably.

I don't know how often I visited them. On my own maybe only two or three times, but those were the most exciting holidays I had. I went by plane from Munich to Copenhagen when I travelled alone, with an orange label round my neck bearing the letters U.M., 'Unaccompanied Minor'. The stewardesses were very nice, I was allowed to go into the cockpit, they gave me toys, and at the end of the flight I went off the plane ahead of everyone else, and drove to the Arrivals area with the stewardesses in a special bus. And then I saw my grandparents through the glass panel: my grandmother in a leather coat with a red headscarf, the dog on a leash, cigarette between her fingers, looking bored. Beside her my grandfather, wearing a hat. He sees me, says something to my grandmother, waves; she looks, sees me too, suddenly laughs, and now she waves as well. The stewardess goes through Customs with me. The sliding door opens, there they are, they are coming towards me, the stewardess lets go of my hand, I run to meet then, the dog is coming closer, there's the dog, I fling myself into my grandmother's arms and breathe in her smoker's smell. Back at last.

‡

On a very rainy summer's day I go to Charlottenlund with my aunt and my cousin. My aunt drives us in her car to the street where my grandparents lived, and we park opposite their house. The garden gate is open, there are brightly coloured plastic toys lying around. We feel a little apprehensive as we get out of the car. So there it is. It's an odd idea to think of someone else living there now, obviously a family with a child. The house is painted white instead of brown. It looks innocent. Just a house.

We stand around outside it slightly too long to be inconspicuous. When we try to look over the fence again we are caught at it by a blonde little girl of about three. She is just coming out of the garden gate, she sees us, and runs back into the house at once. Not long after she comes back in the arms of her mother, who asks us in friendly tones if we are looking for anything.

My cousin explains who we are. The Danes are such nice people; she asks us in.

Inside everything has changed. The entrance hall is carpeted with sisal and almost empty. The living room and dining room are no longer panelled in wood, but painted white, which makes it all look larger and friendlier. Modern furniture, chrome, pale wood. In the bedroom a new window has been added, and an entirely new room has been built on to the back of the house for the children—there are two of them. It looks like something out of a furniture catalogue, a happy home for a young family. That's nice, very nice, and somehow weird.

Before we leave, I peep in at the guest toilet, next to the entrance hall. And suddenly it's all back again. Time seems to have stood still in this little room. The same pale blue tiles as in my grandparents' day—and the same smell. I don't know how that's possible, but the smell of soap and cold smoke has somehow settled between the damp, cold tiles. I close the door, fold the lid of the toilet down and sit on it. A memory of sitting here when my feet couldn't reach the floor...There used to be a little notice on the wall here to the right, at eye level. It said, 'Life Vest Under Your Seat'. My grandfather thought that sort of thing was funny...I open my eyes. It isn't there now.

That evening we sit together at my aunt's dining table for a long time. The atmosphere is of a wake after a funeral. We laugh, drink red wine, look at old photos, remember little details. We remember that my grandmother couldn't ride a bike very well, that she played games of patience in the afternoon, and drank red wine spritzers with her evening meal. At one point my aunt leaves the room for a minute, comes back and puts an A4 folder on the table. She takes out a sheet of paper in my grandmother's handwriting. My aunt hasn't said in advance what it is, and when I realise I get a shock.

It is a Who Gets What list, dated September 1991, so drawn up at least two weeks before their death. It means that they sat together in Copenhagen wondering which of us would like what. Part of their countdown to death. Nothing has been corrected, the writing is tidy, it is their last will and testament.

There were no spectacular riches to be left, only things with a certain value that they were fond of. Jewellery, cufflinks, a collection of antique coins. When my aunt has finished reading the list aloud I go out of the room for a few moments. I want to be alone. I don't know why this material aspect of their departure moves me so much either, since in a way it was all for nothing. My grandfather's pocket watch doesn't mean anything to my brother. My other brother has never worn the cufflinks, they're not his style, and I don't wear the diamond ring. The collection of antique coins left to my cousin has been stolen from his father's safe. My mother was left a necklace that I've never seen her wear. My father was left a ring that is in a bank safe somewhere. They are only things—a ring that doesn't suit me—but suddenly I feel as if they meant more to my grandparents. Something special. Something they loved. And we didn't know how to appreciate them.

‡

In May 1991, five months before their death, my grandparents visited Budapest once more. My father had a concert there, and they were going with him. My mother went too. They had booked into the Radisson Béke, a grand hotel of long, carpeted corridors and gilded charm, about five hundred metres from their old apartment on the Oktogon. I once went there later. Young men in capes and porters' caps stand outside the doorway, smoking, chatting, and showing no inclination to help guests with their luggage.

By now my grandfather must already have been rather weak, but he insisted on going on this trip. My grandmother nagged the doctor until, against his medical judgment, he made out a certificate stating that my grandfather was fit to fly. And so they flew to Budapest.

My mother says the two of them held court in the hotel lounge. They had made themselves look very chic, and received friends there in the afternoon. And my mother reels off a list of several Hungarian names, none of which mean anything to me.

I imagine them seated in the hotel lounge on sofas and chairs with beige upholstery, going through their usual dialogue in front of the waiters carrying pots of coffee round.

Waiter: 'Would you like another coffee?'

'Pista, would we like another coffee?'

'Hm, what do you think? Are you having another coffee?'

'Yes, why not?'

'Well, if you're having another coffee, then so will I.'

'Thank you, yes, we'd like another cup of coffee.'

I know of two photographs from this trip. In one, my grandparents are sitting at a table with my mother and a few old people whom I don't know. My grandmother is less glamorous in the picture than I remember her, she is looking at her inward-turning feet. One hand is on her ashtray, the obligatory lighted cigarette is between her fingers, with the other hand she holds her red handbag firmly on her lap in what looks a slightly anxious or tense way, even if she is laughing in the photo. My grandfather is sitting behind the table. He has his head on one side and is looking, with a sad smile, at two laughing women who are unknown to me. In fact, everyone in this photograph seems relaxed and happy, except my grandparents.

The other photograph shows only my grandfather. It was obviously taken on a café terrace, with a sun umbrella and a waiter in white livery visible in the background. My grandfather is looking at the table in front of him, which is outside the picture. He has raised his bushy white eyebrows, he looks troubled. And his throat is so sinewy and thin as it rises from his shirt that he looks a little like a turtle that has lost its shell.

One evening my grandmother and my father went to the theatre; my grandfather was too weak, my mother not fluent enough in Hungarian—so the two of them spent the evening together, daughter-in-law and father-in-law. They ate in the hotel restaurant, my mother remembers, and had a wonderful evening. He was very charming. A good listener, a courteous table companion, such a delightful person. Did I know that he could make very suggestive remarks?

I think of the white plastic ashtray warning you against too much sex.

When my mother speaks of him she sounds sorry that, ultimately, she knew so little about him, there was so much they never discussed. But then she remembers one of his jokes—do you know what he always said about your grandmother's legs? And I do know, but she tells me all the same. Family stories.

My mother also tells me about a scene that, she thinks,

took place on this trip to Budapest, and which she does not like to remember. A meal with several people present, she doesn't remember who they were. My grandfather, as always immaculately dressed, splashes sauce on his tie. My grandmother scolds him. Can't you be careful, just look what you've done, oh, your nice tie, Pista, do take care! Scolding that dignified elderly gentleman with the white moustache, making him look like a silly little boy in front of everyone.

And she mentions something else—did I know that my grandfather, if other people were around him, always concentrated exclusively on my grandmother? If someone spoke to him or asked him something, it was typical of him to turn to my grandmother asking her, without any apology, 'What's he saying?' As if only she spoke his own language, and no one else would be able to understand him.

What did my grandparents think of Budapest after all those years? Not too much would have changed in the city since 1956—a few more Stalinist blocks of buildings, a few less Jugendstil buildings. Did they feel at home? Did it alienate them to be understood by everyone when they were having a private conversation? In Denmark they were used to discussing, out loud, subjects not meant for other people's ears—if they spoke Hungarian, no one could understand them. So they would stand in the supermarket or sit in the restaurant making disparaging remarks about those around them to their heart's content. More precisely, of course only my grandmother made the disparaging remarks while my grandfather agreed with her, both in normal conversational tones. It had been known for someone to turn round and address a remark to them in Hungarian, but not often enough to break them of the habit.

After the trip my grandfather told the Danish doctor, who was greatly relieved to see him safely back in Denmark, about the trip. It had brought everything full circle, he said. He had heard a recital given by his son in his homeland, and now it was finished. 'It is finished,' the doctor tells me he said, those very words. 'He said them like Jesus on the Cross.'

Back in Copenhagen, my grandfather's health was deteriorating. Within a few weeks he had lost twelve kilos. He was tired all the time, especially in the morning; he felt a little better after breakfast. In the evening he had sudden outbreaks of sweating, he slept poorly and woke up several times in the night, which had never happened before. And he was downcast, even sad. That too was most unusual for him. He had been even-tempered all his life (except when he happened to be driving a car). At the end of August he consulted a doctor, who said he was in a state of depression that could be a side-effect of his sleeping tablets. The doctor's written diagnosis, which was among my grandfather's papers, finds nothing wrong with his mind, but says his depression was the result of his physical weakness. He was approaching his end. He knew it would not be long now.

‡

The day before my grandparents took their lives, on 12 October 1991, my other cousin visited them. It was already dark when she arrived that afternoon—autumn days are short in Denmark—and she did not see my grandfather. He was asleep, said my grandmother, but she should send her love.

My cousin does not like to remember that visit. It was depressing, she says, our grandmother seemed sad. It can of course be that in my cousin's memory she seemed sad only in retrospect, but when my cousin talks about it she gives herself a little shake as if to rid herself of something unpleasant, and concludes with an apologetic laugh.

She sat on the living-room sofa, she says, my grand-mother had put on a record, or rather put *in* a record, because they had a modern Bang & Olufsen record player with a tray on which the discs slid soundlessly in and out. I remember that you could see through the brown Perspex lid and watch the stylus arm automatically position itself and drop the stylus into the groove; there was something futuristic about it that impressed me greatly. Then my grandmother sat down on the sofa beside her. She had put on Wagner, the 'Liebestod' from *Tristan and Isolde*. It was dark outside, my grandfather was asleep, a red standard lamp was on and spread a little warm light. The singer began, as if from afar the sound of a clarinet rose softly, then strings. My cousin didn't under- stand the German words, but it seemed to be about something sad, a kind of long-drawn-out sigh rising higher and higher, and the orchestra matched it with increasing urgency. My grandmother seemed determined to hear the whole of the 'Liebestod'. She sat there calmly, upright as ever, her dog had jumped up on the sofa beside her, and she stroked the dog's head slowly and said nothing. Not for a full eight minutes, or however long the aria took in the recording that my grandparents owned. My cousin found the situation uncomfortable, and unusually serious for my grandmother, who usually preferred a chat. 'Have you seen *Dirty Dancing*, did you like it?' 'What do you think of King Ludwig II of Bavaria and his castle of Neuschwanstein?' She liked to discuss such subjects.

When the last bar died away my grandmother rose to her feet, went over to the record player, made the control take the stylus arm back to the beginning, and Isolde's 'Liebestod' began all over again. This time my grandmother remained standing by the record player. That sad melody again, the vocal line very simple, like a child's lullaby, then strings playing tremolo, horns, the singer's voice rising higher and higher, its vibrato encompassing several notes. A sudden switch into the minor key.

'Do you know the story of Tristan and Isolde?' asked my grandmother, turning the volume down.

My cousin shook her head. 'No.'

My grandmother told her the plot of the tragedy. How Tristan died, and how Isolde, in her great love for him, looks at him in death as she stands beside the body of her beloved— and feels joy, great joy!

Isolde sings: 'Mild and gentle see him smile, see him open his fair eyes, oh see him, friends, do you not see? Ever lighter see him shine, see him rise in radiant starlight!'

My grandmother turns the sound down again. Isolde loves Tristan so much that she doesn't want to live without him, she tells my cousin.

My cousin, sixteen years old at the time, feels that all this is beyond her. The whole thing makes her feel uneasy. She doesn't understand why our grandmother is delivering this lecture to her. She doesn't understand what my grand-mother wants her to do. Was there something else coming? Did she want to go to the opera with her, and this was a way of preparing her?

'Ah, to drown—to sink down—this is joy—unalloyed,' sings Isolde.

'She follows him into death,' says my grandmother.

'Listen—the poison has taken effect now, listen to the lovely music, and now she's dead.'

My cousin tries to look as interested as she can. She is afraid that my grandmother will bring the stylus arm down at the start for the third time. But after the last bar has died away again, my grandmother turns off the loudspeakers and says cheerfully, 'Come along, let's play cards. After last time our score's two-one to me.'

‡

When I was little I drew up a secret list of which of my grandparents would die first. In fact I drew it up the other way around, since the list was the outcome of love and fear. First place, therefore, went to whichever I wanted to live longest. I was about six or seven at the time, and expected my grandmothers and grandfathers to die any moment now, they all seemed to me so old. Their approaching death was always before my eyes, and I took precautions. You'll leave me that, won't you? I asked my Heidelberg grandmother every time I saw her, pointing to the gold bracelet she always wore, and she laughed and said yes. She was just sixty at the time and in the best of health.

My Heidelberg grandmother, my mother's mother, came first on my secret list. I wanted her to be the last of my four grandparents to die, if she had to die at all, which I would have tried to prevent by any conceivable means if that had been possible. I would even have given up the gold bracelet to keep her alive. My Heidelberg grandmother was such a small woman that when I was just ten I could already look her straight in the eye, and she was such a dear that I thought she deserved a very long life. Second on the list was my Copenhagen grandfather, the most patient, good-natured person in my own little world. Third was my Heidelberg grandfather, a distinguished and cultured man who could be wonderfully silly with his grandchildren. And last came my Copenhagen grandmother—to whom I really felt so close. So mine was a sad list as well as a particularly macabre one because it reveals not just my childish arrogance but my scale of values, in which my Copenhagen grandmother, whom I apparently resembled so much, came so far down in my estimation. She was temperamental, unpredictable and egotistic. Just like me, so I felt she should be punished for it.

And then it all turned out very differently. My beloved little Heidelberg grandmother was the first to die. She fell down dead one day hanging out the washing. Then my Copenhagen grandparents died; they died at the same time, on the same day, in the same hour. Much later my Heidelberg grandfather died. There was no fourth place.

‡

How do two people feel on their last day alive? Do they think that everything they do is for the last time? The last time working in the garden, the last glass of milk, the last time they will ever clean their teeth? Or have they already put such thoughts behind them on that day? Have they privately said goodbye in the last few weeks and months to all the things that make up life, both good and bad, and do they forbid themselves such thoughts at the end and live exactly as they did before, until the hour comes when they have planned to die?

I have often wondered how my grandparents behaved on the day of their death. Did they shed tears? Were they on edge? Tense? Quiet? The fact that there were two of them must have made it all a little easier. A trouble shared is a trouble halved. But is that true? Was it true for both of them?

Everyone to whom I have talked about my grandparents' death shared my opinion that it was my grandmother's idea, her own wish and her plan to take her life together with my grandfather. Many of them were convinced that she had had that plan in mind for a long time. And no one could have dissuaded her, not even my grandfather who, as they all agree, would have opposed it for a long time, only to give in to her in the end. As usual.

The death announcement printed in a Danish newspaper, which might well raise questions in the minds of outsiders because of their identical day of death, said, 'The answer is their great love.' That is the gentlest way of referring to the double suicide. But is it the whole truth? Does not their death, above all, suggest fear? A woman's fear of being unloved, alone, a burden on others, perhaps sick and frail herself some day? And was there not also a considerable amount of aggression in behaving, so far as her own children were concerned, as if she were entirely alone in the world?

‡

My grandfather is still sitting on the sofa. He is holding the book *Final Exit*, but he has let it sink to his lap, and has closed his eyes.

My grandmother enters the room.

'Why are you sitting in the dark?' she says, switching on the standard lamp beside the sofa. She has a pad of paper and a pen in her hands.

My grandfather opens his eyes.

'And what do they say about it?' She sits down beside him.

He doesn't seem to know what she means.

'It must be more certain by injection, don't you think? That way it goes straight into the bloodstream. It's logical.'

'Hm.' My grandfather picks up the book, looks at it, turns the pages.

'The only thing against it,' my grandmother goes on, 'is that I don't know whether I'd be quick enough. I'd give you the injection first, and inject myself second. I really don't know—what do you think? How many seconds before the drug works?'

My grandfather looks back a few pages. 'Where was it...' he murmurs.

'But it's definitely more certain.' My grandmother seems to be talking to herself. 'Much more direct. Otherwise it could take—what do you think, a minute? Longer? Not much longer, it tells you all about it in there, no, show me the book, where is it? Where are you looking?'

She takes the book from his hands, and he lets her.

'I'm wondering,' she says, turning the pages rapidly a few times, 'whether I shouldn't give you an injection and then drink it myself, I just wish I knew how long...ah, here we are.'

'I'm not in favour of an injection,' says my grandfather. 'Let's do it exactly the way we decided.'

My grandmother runs her finger along the lines. 'Injection is the perfect way, of course, but...hm, hm, hm.'

'We don't want to run any risks,' said my grandfather.

'Exactly,' says my grandmother, reading the English text again. 'Time in coma usually one minute, average five point six minutes—'

The telephone rings.

My grandmother is so startled that she jumps.

'Who can that be?' asks my grandfather.

'How should I know?' asks my grandmother, only now noticing how tense she feels.

The telephone rings again. The ring tone seems to her very loud and shrill. As if someone wanted to disturb her.

'Perhaps it's something about the dog,' says my grandfather.

'Perhaps. Or maybe it's Sebastian again. Or the family in Munich. Or someone has just dialled the wrong number.' My grandmother is all on edge now.

The phone rings a couple more times and then falls silent.

'I'm sure it was something about the dog,' says my grandfather.

'It can't have been, Pista! Think about it, why would Inga call us here? If it was something about the dog she'd call Munich, Pista, she has the number, why would she call here? Why?'

My grandmother slams the book down on the coffee table.

'And why would it be anything about the dog? What would be the matter with the dog? The dog is fine. She was fine this morning, she was fine at midday, why would it be any different now?'

My grandfather reaches for the book.

'Maybe we forgot to give Inga the basket, or something else is…'

'We didn't forget, Pista, we thought of everything.' My grandmother's voice is louder now, although she didn't mean to raise it. 'While you were having a nice rest I packed it all up, the basket and the dog food, her leash, her brush, Pista, don't you understand that? That's why we took Mitzi to Inga's.'

My grandmother props her chin in her hands and looks as if she is trying to calm down. Twenty-one, twenty-two…

'Well, have you decided?' asks my grandfather.

My grandmother takes a packet of Prince Denmark cigarettes out of her pocket and lights one. She draws deeply on it.

'You're right, we'll do it the way we planned,' she says. 'I'm just afraid you'll die too fast. I don't want to be alone.'

She stands up quickly. As she leaves the room she switches the light on.

‡

My aunt and I are at a residential home in Copenhagen, visiting two women who used to be friends of my grand-mother's and went to her exercise classes for seniors. One of them, Clara, is ninety and has been living here for a few years now, the other, Margarete, is eighty-two and moved in only a few weeks ago.

They both look as if they had spent long periods of their lives in the open air—their skin is slightly tanned and shows age spots, their hair is white, both have bright blue eyes and a hearty laugh. We meet in Margarete's room in the home for seniors and have to leave it again at once, because it is lunchtime, and the dining room is some way off. They have a very strict timetable here, says Clara, picking up her walking-stick; she speaks to my aunt, who translates for me.

We take the lift, which is well-equipped with rails for the disabled. Once on the ground floor we go down a long corridor. Linoleum flooring. We overtake a few people shuffling slowly along behind wheeled Zimmer frames. Everyone is wearing slippers. The wheels squeak on the linoleum.

The dining room could be in a youth hostel, except that everyone here is old. Blue trays, fibrous meat, mashed potato and canned peas. Clara and Margarete eat very cautiously, morsel after morsel, chewing for a long time. Later we drink tea from blue and white Copenhagen porcelain up in Margarete's room. We make small-talk, and I am glad that my aunt came with me, because it means they can speak Danish together, and then she translates for me, and in between I pause and try to guess what they are talking about. Something to do with grandchildren, the advantages of this seniors' residential home, the particularly mild autumn this year. The afternoon drags on, time doesn't seem to be passing at all, five minutes, ten minutes, an eternity. Even Clara's earlobes are wrinkled. She has many liver spots, and by comparison Margarete almost looks still young—almost. We also talk about my grandparents. Vera—a dear friend, such an impressive personality, what a couple. They used to talk about music a lot, both ladies say, about concerts, the opera, the cultural life of Copenhagen. And then the end... they both shake their heads.

I don't feel as if these two women, pleasant as they are, can tell me anything about my grandparents that I didn't already know. More likely they are members of the Copenhagen audience for which my grandparents used to perform their party number: the interesting, fascinating, music-loving couple. My grandmother, chatting in friendly tones, kept the audience at a distance, showed them the glittering surface of her life, smoked cigarettes as she talked and looked fabulous. It was the role of her life, and she never fluffed a line.

I try to imagine what it would be like if there had never been a suicide. My grandfather would have died a natural death in the spring of 1992. And my grandmother would be as old as Clara and Margarete today. Would she, too, be living in a residential home? Perhaps in this one, which has a good reputation?

As we leave, I think, I can understand my grand-mother.

‡

About six weeks before their death my grandmother dropped in unannounced to see my aunt. That was very unusual, because they were not on the best of terms at this time. Also, my grandmother didn't like driving the car, and she had never before, without previous arrangement, come from Charlottenlund to Lyngby, a little way north of Copenhagen, where my aunt was living at the time—to ring the bell and say she was just calling in to see if there was anyone at home. So my aunt was surprised to hear her mother's deep voice through the intercom, asking if she could come up. She had brought strawberry cake from the patisserie, the best there was, says my aunt. Are you cross with me? she said instead of a greeting. And she told my aunt she should visit her father because he was in a very bad way.

So a little later my aunt went to Charlottenlund. She was alarmed when she saw my grandfather. He was so thin. He was lying in bed with an oxygen inhaler beside him. His breathing was heavy, and he was very tired. They talked briefly, not about anything real and important, then he wanted to sleep. My aunt doesn't remember what she had expected, only that she was disappointed when she left.

That was at the beginning of September.

In their last weeks and months they were gradually saying goodbye to us all, even if it was only in retrospect that we understood that, or wanted to understand it.

For my birthday at the end of September, my grandparents sent me an envelope containing a thousand-mark note inside a card. A thousand marks! I had never even known before what colour a thousand-mark note was (brown). I was to buy myself something nice with it, they had written in the card in my grandfather's handwriting, something that would always remind me of them. Then they turned to more important matters: 'We always got on well. You are very dear to us.' And finally they sent me 'every good wish for the years to come, with all our love.'

Could they have said it more clearly?

In my diary for 1991 I can see what I made of it at the time. I knew that my grandfather was very ill, and that the wording in the card sounded like a goodbye, but I didn't think my grandmother would go through with the plan that she had confided to my parents. My mother told me about it at the time. She was worried about my grandmother, she told me, she meant to take her own life if my grandfather died but, said my mother—and I still remember this conversation very well—she herself had told my grandmother that she was welcome to come and live with us in Munich, and that seemed to have solved the problem. Or at least postponed it. 'She likes high drama and she likes to put on an act,' I wrote at the time in my diary, reassuring myself.

On the evening when my grandparents took their own lives in Copenhagen, a girlfriend had invited me and a few other people to supper in Munich. It was the very same evening, 13 October 1991, I still have my calendar for that year. I remember telling the company around the table that we were worried. That my grandfather was very ill, dying, and my grandmother had said she didn't want to live a day longer after he died. They were planning to kill themselves, I said. I told them just like that, sitting at the table when the pasta was being cleared away. I remember that I felt bad the moment I had said it. I remember I suddenly thought, this is too private, I ought to have kept it to myself. But by then it was out. And I realised that the subject fascinated the others. I remember how they listened with interest and asked questions. It was what you might call a good party subject. And it wasn't certain that they were going to kill themselves. It was really much more likely that they were simply toying with the idea, had merely raised the subject in passing, but my grandmother knew she could come and live with us in Munich any time she liked. Or with Erzsi in America. And after all, no one knew when the moment would come. if it ever did come to that. Which one hoped it never would. It was only a story, only a good story. That's what I told myself. And so what should we have done?

‡

My father has told me about a box of my grandfather's papers that he keeps in a drawer somewhere. It was in this box that he found the document showing that my grandfather had been liberated not from Mauthausen but from Gunskirchen. He himself doesn't know exactly what else is in the box, they're just papers of some kind, he says, papers that were lying around my grandparents' house when he came to Copenhagen after their death to wind up their estate. He simply took a few of them, put them away and never looked at them again. And now we are sitting at my parents' kitchen table with that box in front of us. Its lid doesn't fit because it is too full of papers.

On top is a packet of letters addressed to my father. They are the condolences he received after my grandparents' death. We put them to one side. Underneath them is my grandparents' last tax return. That's not so interesting either, we think. Under that, a letter from the faculty of medicine at Szeged University, from which we gather that my grandfather was bequeathing to it his professional library, including twenty-seven years of issues of the *Journal of Bone and Joint Surgery*. Gradually we take out everything. Passport pictures of my grandfather from various decades, wearing glasses in various fashions of frames. Portrait photographs of my grandfather as a child, a calendar that was hanging in their kitchen in the year of their death, but with only birthdays marked, and almost every week the note 'Concert'.

Then my father takes a newspaper cutting out of the box. It is clearly part of the front page of the newspaper that my grandparents subscribed to, the *Berlingske Tidende*, and is a short report from the news columns. 'Håndbog i selvmord', is the headline, underlined in pencil. It's the article in which they learned of the existence of the book. They had torn it out of the paper and kept it, and for some reason my father packed it in the box and now I have it in my hands, the original article that helped my grandparents to die. The text says that a book has been published in the United States, a suicide manual. It is called *Final Exit,* and it is top of the *New York Times* bestseller list. Someone, I assume my grandmother, circled the title of the book in pencil, underlined the author's name three lines further down, and joined up the pencil markings with a geometric pattern around the edge, the kind you might doodle in noting down a phone number. She also drew a kind of large onion shape beside the headline; perhaps a variation on the playing card symbol for spades. Its rounded area has been hatched in so that it looks three-dimensional.

We have found something else in the box: a little piece

of paper on which my grandmother has noted something in Hungarian. The following points are listed, one above another:

- 6 p.m., weak tea and toast;
- 7 p.m., anti-emetic, normal dose;
- 7.30 p.m., sleeping tablets.

She wrote it in her angular script, in which she had also entered our birthdays on the kitchen calendar. A perfectly normal to-do list for their suicide.

‡

My grandmother is sitting on the red sofa, which has cushions so soft that you always sink a little too far into them to get up again without an effort. She is doing a box up in gift-wrapping paper. There are Santa Clauses printed on the paper; it dates from last Christmas, but that doesn't bother her. After all, it will soon be Christmas again. She holds a lighted cigarette, almost half burnt down, between the fingers of her left hand. A few other presents, already gift-wrapped, lie on the coffee table. So do more sheets of wrapping paper, all of them folded up once and then smoothed out again, along with sticky tape and a pair of scissors. Also a few objects. A transparent plastic box containing coins. A pair of cufflinks on a silk cushion in a small box. A gold pocket watch.

From his armchair, my grandfather watches her tie a gold bow around the finished parcel. She pulls the ends of the ribbon sharply over the blades of the scissors a couple of times to make them curl. When she has finished she puts it with the other presents.

'Pretty,' says my grandfather.

My grandmother picks up the box of coins.

'Who's getting your ring?' asks my grandfather. My grandmother looks up.

'What ring do you mean?'

'The one you're wearing.'

'Erzsi,' says my grandmother, knocking the ash off her cigarette—it's a wonder that it stayed there so long—and extracts a sheet of red and white striped paper from the pile. She seems to think this one is the right size.

'What about my watch?'

'What?' She puts the box on the paper and folds the ends over experimentally. Yes, it fits.

'My watch, who's getting that?'

'Your watch?' my grandmother casts him a glance saying: we've discussed that so often, please think about it for yourself. She folds the red and white striped paper neatly round the box and puts the ashtray on top of it to keep the paper from unfolding again. A short puff of her cigarette and then she reaches for the roll of sticky tape.

'We can have something to eat soon,' she says.

'I'm not hungry,' he says.

'No. Nor am I.' She holds the sticky tape a little further away from her eyes. 'But we have to eat something.' Oh, where was the beginning of this tape? She turns the roll round again, slowly.

'What's the time?'

'You want me to unpack the watch again, Pista? I don't know. Five o'clock?'

She has found the end of the tape now, and scrapes some of it off the roll with her fingernail.

'Is there anything I can do to help you?' he says. He asks out of politeness. He himself has no idea what he could really do to help.

She pulls out a length of sticky tape, bites it sideways and tears it off. 'You can put some music on,' she says. She presses the sticky tape down over the wrapping paper. 'But not Wagner, please. Something light.'

She draws on her cigarette one last time—it has now burnt down to the filter—and crushes it out in the ashtray. Then she picks up the box of cufflinks. My grandfather stands up and goes over to the shelf of records, which has acquired more and more CDs over the last two years. A little later the sound of brass fills the room, rising in melodious harmony with long crescendo passages. It is rather emotional, but that is just what my grandmother likes. This is one of her favourite works, Ferenc Erkel's *Hunyadi László*, a very Hungarian, very late Romantic opera. 'Telj-múlj, nagy idö / Ez, mit ma lelkünk úgy remél,' sings the chorus from the loudspeakers. 'Pass by us, time, great time / our souls long for that today.' Usually my grandmother hums along a couple of octaves lower, but today she goes on packing up presents in silence, and my grandfather watches her from his armchair.

‡

A few days before their suicide the doctor who was friends with my grandparents visited them. They had phoned to invite him to come by, saying nothing more precise. He knew they were toying with the idea of taking their own lives— this was the same doctor whom they had asked to get them a copy of *Final Exit*, and who had not been willing to comply with their wish. He didn't know if they wanted to see him as a friend or a doctor, probably both, he thought.

I visit him in Copenhagen, where he lives with his wife in a beautiful, light house with a garden; the sea is not far away, you can smell it. His wife has made lunch for us: cucumber salad, prawns, mild yellow hard cheese, cooked ham, black bread and salted butter. *Frokost*. As in my grandparents' house.

We skip the preliminaries and begin talking about them at once. He tells me that at this last meeting he thought they were both in good spirits. Of course he doesn't know what the cheerfulness might have concealed, he had not known anything private about the two of them. My grandmother opened the door to him, he says, my grandfather had been sitting on the living-room sofa, very thin, tired, but to all appearances not depressed. Not outwardly anyway. After they had talked about this and that for a while, my grandfather suddenly reached behind him and, with a triumphant 'We got it!', brought out *Final Exit* from behind a cushion.

Knud, the doctor, speaks very warmly of my grandparents. He describes them as an 'aristocratic couple', calls them 'king and queen', his wife and he had liked them very much. I have an idea that of all the people I am speaking to, he is the only one—apart from Erzsi—to have seen behind the façade that my grandparents erected. To have been aware that there even was a façade. I can speak frankly with him, I feel. My grandparents had been able to speak frankly with him as well.

My grandfather had asked him, he tells me, whether it was really necessary to take an anti-emetic to prevent vomiting. So he decided that at this point he would tell them everything they ought to consider. He hadn't wanted to help them on their way to death, but when he saw that they were going to do it anyway, even without his help, he wanted to enable them to leave life as easily and painlessly as possible.

'I couldn't bear the idea of only one of them surviving,' he says, 'possibly badly injured.'

So he answered my grandfather's questions to the best of his knowledge and as best his conscience would allow. It had been a professional conversation, he remembers. Two doctors in discussion with each other. Yes, the anti-emetic was absolutely necessary. Yes, the poison would work faster if the gelatine capsule was removed and only the powder taken, that was a good idea.

Knud says he had the impression that there was a pact between my grandparents for neither to die without the other. A solemn promise that they had made long ago, maybe fifty years ago, after the end of the Second World War, and perhaps they had renewed it after their flight from Hungary. I think exactly the same, but Knud doesn't know that. Their decision had been final, he says. There was no doubt about it.

When he left, my grandfather stayed sitting there, my grandmother went to the door with him. In the hall he asked her whether she wouldn't think it over again. She was perfectly healthy, he pointed out, she could live for a long time yet. 'You're a coward,' she told him, laughing. 'A nice man but a coward. Cowards don't dare to look death in the face.' Then, he says, she told him not to worry, they weren't going to do it the next day. And when he turned once more at the garden gate, she was still standing in the doorway waving to him and smiling.

Four days later they were dead.

Did my grandmother close the door after him and go back into the living room shaking her head: such a handsome man—as she did indeed think—it's just a pity he is such a coward? Or after she had shut the door behind him did her cheerful mood, which perhaps was merely assumed for their guest, give way to determined action?

Did you note it all down, Pista? What did he say, how much of the anti-emetic?

That same afternoon my grandmother went to the pharmacy in Ordrup, not far from Charlottenlund, and bought a packet of painkillers prescribed for rheumatic disorders. An overdose leads to respiratory depression and cardiac arrest. She bought a hundred 115 milligram capsules. My grandfather had made out the prescription.

‡

My grandmother is sitting in the bedroom on her side of the bed, the right-hand side, the curtains are drawn, the balloon-shaped ceiling lamp bathes the room in milky white light. She has picked up a framed photo from the bedside table. It shows my grandmother herself as a small child. She looks like a gypsy boy, black eyes, short black hair, thick fringe. The man smiling at her so kindly from the side is her father, Elémer, a rotund little man with a bald patch and a black moustache, smiling at the camera. A little way to one side, wearing a long, black dress, stands a beautiful woman with long black hair and a melancholy expression—Gizella. My grandmother looks at it for a moment. Then she puts it back on the bedside table. For the very first time she regrets believing in nothing but herself. How much easier it must be for people who have a God, she thinks. Those weak but lucky characters can indulge in the superstition that death is not the end of everything. Cowards, she thinks. They dare not contemplate the worms that will bore through their coffins and turn their remains into compost. Her thoughts go to her two children, but she does not allow herself to soften. They're grown up, she thinks. They've had families of their own for years. They can't expect her to stay alive for their sake now. It was her life. She owed no one anything. They'll understand that, she decides.

It is very quiet except for the ticking of the alarm clocks on their two bedside tables. Can't Pista put some music on, does he have to surround himself with silence now, of all times? She would like to hear something other than her own thoughts, which keep chasing each other at high speed. Where did she put her cigarettes, ah, here, and where's her lighter? A few days ago parts of the Old Town of Dubrovnik were destroyed by a bombing raid, she has seen pictures of it on the news. As a child she went to Dubrovnik with her parents once or twice. Suddenly she misses the dog. Mitzi, she thinks, little Mitzi. What is she doing now? Would Inga offer her a good home? Would she be able to stay there permanently? When would someone notice that...

'Vera?' he calls from the living room.

Oh dear, what was it now? Couldn't he be left alone for a second? Sometimes he was like a small child.

'Vera?' His voice is a little louder now.

She lights a cigarette, draws deeply on it. 'Yes?' She stands up.

‡

My grandfather is lying on the living-room sofa, his head on one of its arms, puffing a cigarillo and watching the smoke rise and disperse in the air just below the ceiling. So today is the day when he is going to die. Was it a good life? Yes, he thinks. It was a good life.

'Vera?' he calls.

No reply.

'Vera?' he calls again.

'Yes?' she replies slowly.

'What are you doing?'

No answer.

He is just about to repeat what he said when he hears her footsteps in the corridor that links the bedroom and bathroom to the kitchen, from which in turn you get into the living room. He draws on the cigarillo. The temperature in the room is pleasant. He feels no pain at the moment, he is just a little queasy with hunger, but they will soon be eating something, he won't have to wait for long.

My grandmother comes into the room, her cigarette between her fingers.

'What is it?' she asks.

'I was wondering where you were.'

'I was tidying something up,' says my grandmother.

'You're wearing your gold necklace,' says my grandfather. 'Come along, sit down here with me.'

He raises his head, takes his legs off the cushions and sits up, not quite as vigorously as he had hoped to. He is weaker than he feels after all. My grandmother stands in the middle of the room, undecided.

'Come along,' says my grandfather again, patting the place on the sofa beside him.

'I'd like us to agree on something,' she says, and stays where she is.

My grandfather looks at her.

'Today is a perfectly normal day. We're only going to bed.'

'To sleep a little longer than usual?' He makes it sound amusing.

'We're just going to sleep. Nothing dramatic. Agreed?'

'Come here to me.' My grandfather puts his arm out to her.

'Well? Can we agree on that?' She takes a few steps towards the sofa.

'Yes.'

'Yes what?'

'Today is a perfectly normal day. Maybe we'll watch the news...no, no news? What are you planning to do, then? Come on. A perfectly normal day. We'll be going to bed soon. I'm very tired already. A perfectly normal day.'

My grandfather leans slightly forward, and draws my grandmother towards him by the hand in which she isn't holding a cigarette. She gives way, sits down on the sofa beside him and puts her head on his shoulder. He strokes her dark grey hair a few times—it feels like steel wool—and then she frees herself from his touch.

'We still have a lot to do,' she says.

'Of course,' says my grandfather. 'What's the time?'

‡

In the kitchen, my grandmother runs water until it is warm and then fills the kettle and puts it on the stove. She checks that the whistle is on firmly enough—sometimes it is too loose, then no sound comes out, and more than once all the water had evaporated by the time she finally went to see if it was boiling yet.

She takes two cups out of the cupboard. Not the best cups with the gold rims, but ordinary white cups with curving sides, and hangs a teabag in each, Earl Grey. Then she goes to the breadbox and takes out the packet of toasting bread that she bought yesterday. It is still unopened. She undoes the little metal twist at the top and takes out two slices. She thinks for a moment and then takes out a third and a fourth. It is white bread, so there won't be much roughage, and she remembers that their stomachs shouldn't be too empty.

She puts all four slices at once into the toaster, which is big enough to take another four. Before she can switch it on she has to plug it in—she takes the plug out of the socket every time she has used the toaster, because of what she herself knows is a totally irrational fear that electrical gadgets might start up of their own accord and set the house on fire some day. She presses down the lever; a moment later the elements are glowing, and warmth rises from the toaster. For a little while she thinks of nothing, and then the whistle on the kettle begins that quiet whispering with which it announces that it will be whistling full strength any moment now, so the water is about to boil. And as she pours the simmering water into the teacups the toaster clicks, and the four slices of toasted bread pop up.

My grandmother takes two little wooden boards off the drainer and puts the slices of toast on them. They are done just right—nice and brown in the middle, a little paler round the edges. She opens the cutlery drawer and takes out a wooden butter-knife, then she gets a tub of margarine out of the fridge and begins spreading margarine on the toast. It melts quickly. She spreads it neatly out to the sides. When she closes the lid of the tub again, her eye falls on the use-by date printed on it. 'If chilled will keep to January 1992,' it says. Until next year, that is. She finds that a comforting idea. The world would go on turning.

At 6.30 my grandparents, sitting on the sofa, eat two slices of toast and margarine each and drink a cup of weak tea without milk. My grandmother suddenly feels strangely cheerful. As if now that they have reached the first point on her to-do list, nothing can go wrong. As if they had come into the finishing straight, and from this point it would all be as they had planned it for so long. From now on she doesn't have to think any more, only to act. From now on she knows what has to be done, and when. She takes Pista's hand and squeezes it for

a moment. He looks at her and nods, almost imperceptibly, and laughter rises in her throat, and it isn't so easy to swallow it again.

‡

At 6.45 my grandmother goes all round the house, putting the lights on in all the rooms and drawing the curtains. She is making as much noise about it as she can, treading firmly, muttering remarks like, 'There,' and 'There we are, then.' The house seems to her strangely quiet without a dog. Not what she's used to. Not really comfortable. She puts on light after light, rearranges a cushion here and there, moves her black coat from the coat-stand in the hall and hangs it in the guestroom wardrobe after all. 'There.'

When she comes back from her little tour and goes into the bedroom, my grandfather is already wearing the striped pyjamas she has put out for him. He is sitting on the bed.

'Pista,' she says, sounding almost excited. 'You must come and look. Come on, let's go round the rooms once more.'

She suddenly has a kind of festive feeling. The whole house is brightly lit. And so beautifully neat and tidy. And the roses in the living room smell so lovely. This is just how she always wanted it to be. Light. Bright. Clear.

My grandfather shakes his head. He doesn't want to stand up again, and even if he did want to, just now he can't.

'I've put all the lights on,' says my grandmother. 'It's beautiful.'

'You've done what?'

My grandfather can hardly make out what his wife is saying. His mind is so dulled. Is it agitation? Fear? Probably weariness. He has been sleeping all day recently because of lying awake at night. And today he even went out of doors. He feels as if a leaden weight were pressing him down, and he has no strength to brace himself against it.

'You've done what?' he repeats quietly.

My grandmother sits down on the bed beside him and takes his hand.

'It doesn't matter,' she says. 'Everything's all right.'

‡

At seven o'clock my grandmother gives my grandfather, who is in bed, two anti-emetic tablets. She herself has already swallowed two in the bathroom. By now she has made herself ready for the night. She has applied a little rouge, only a touch so that it won't rub off on the bedclothes. She has brushed her hair and put on her best nightdress. It is white silk, with a girlish frill at the collar. The silk is very light-weight, she hardly feels it. She has put on jewellery. Her mother's gold necklace round her neck, her delicate gold watch on her wrist. She has taken off the gold ring that she normally wears all the time, three intertwining circles, and put it on the bedside table. The ring is for Erzsi, and she already feels that it is no longer hers.

'Do you need water?' asks my grandmother.

My grandfather shakes his head.

‡

Her gold watch says five past seven. My grandmother is sitting on the bed beside my grandfather, looking at him and stroking his hand. The mechanical nature of the movement calms her. It is like stroking herself. He is breathing heavily, she doesn't know if he is asleep, but she doesn't want to wake him. The list saying what to do lies on her desk. She can see it from the bed, but she doesn't need to. She knows it by heart. Anyway there is only one point left on it. She strokes her husband's forehead. It is very cold and slightly moist with sweat. She looks at her watch again. It is still five past seven.

‡

At 7.25 my grandmother gets to her feet. She would like company now after all.

'Pista.'

My grandfather makes a sound and opens his eyes. For a brief moment he looks as if he doesn't know where he is.

'It's nearly half past,' says my grandmother.

'Hm,' says my grandfather.

'Pista,' she says again, more urgently. 'It's nearly half past. Please, I don't want to be alone now.'

'I'm here,' says my grandfather, fighting his weariness with all the strength he can muster and sitting up.

'Good.' She walks round the bed to her bedside table and takes a packet of tablets out of the drawer.

'Are you still there?' she asks, without turning round.

'Hm,' says my grandfather. 'What's the time?' He looks a little like a schoolboy in his pyjamas with their broad stripes.

'Seven-thirty. We're going to take the sleeping tablets now.'

'Already?' says my grandfather.

'Pista, it's seven-thirty.' She sounds just as irritated as on any other day.

Walking round the bed again, she counts out a few tablets and puts them in my grandfather's outstretched hand, passing him a glass of water that had also been standing ready on her bedside table. My grandfather puts all the tablets in his mouth at once. He has to wash them down several times before he has swallowed them all. My grandmother goes back to her bedside table and puts the tablets she has counted out for herself in her hand. She swallows them one by one, with a small sip of water each time.

'There,' she says, when she has finished.

'Have you written the letter yet?' asks my grandfather.

'No, that comes next,' she says. This is the sequence of events: anti-emetic, sleeping tablets, letter. Paper and pen are lying ready on her bedside table.

She sits on the bed. 'You write.' She gives him the pen.

My grandfather picks up a book lying on his bedside table to rest the paper on it.

'What do I write?'

'Pista, what we discussed. You write the kind of thing one's supposed to write. As it says in the book. Shall I fetch the book?'

'No, I remember now.'

He puts pen to paper and begins to write. 'This has been well-considered.' He writes it in Danish. 'Dette er blevet velovervejet.'

'And say that you wrote the prescription for the drugs,' she says.

'Jeg har skabt medicinen...' he continues writing.

'And that it was done without help from anyone else.'

He nods. He writes slowly but continuously.

She turns back to her bedside table and from the drawer takes a small block of Post-it Notes, a free gift advertising a medical supplies firm, on which she sometimes jots down things that occur to her before she goes to sleep and that she doesn't want to forget. She takes her fountain pen and writes on the top note:

'Please do not try to revive us.'

Then she adds the date and her signature, and tears the note off.

'There,' she says—as if she were ticking something off a list.

She stands up, goes the few steps to the door that is standing open, and sticks the Post-it Note on the door outside the room at eye level. After running her knuckles once or twice over the adhesive strip at the back, to make sure it will stay in place, she goes back to the bed.

My grandfather is still writing.

'Where have you got to?' she asks.

'Jeg er så forpint af min sygdom,' he reads aloud. 'How do you spell cardiomyopathy in Danish?'

'With an "i" at the end,' she says.

The little advertising block of Post-it Notes is still on her bedside table. She takes her fountain pen and writes something. 'We have lived together, we are dying together. We have loved you very much. Mami.' She writes it in Hungarian, it sounds like a poem: 'Együtt éltünk. Együtt megyünk. Szerettünk titeket nagyon. Mami.'

Then she puts the cap on her pen again. Is it normal that

she doesn't feel the effects of the sleeping tablets yet? How long before they make her feel tired?

'Finished,' says my grandfather.

He holds the sheet of paper out to my grandmother, who takes it and reads it aloud.

'Dette er blevet velovervejet. Jeg har skabt medicinen. Ingen kan vaere ansvarlig for hvad der er sket. Jeg er så forpint af min sygdom (kardiomyopathi)...at alt hvad jeg ønsker risikerer er en fredelig afsked fra livet.' And his signature.

He has written it on the back of the *American Journal of Medicine*. His handwriting is shaky. My grandmother is satisfied.

'I'll be back in a minute.' She takes his letter and her own note into the living room. She puts my grandfather's letter on the coffee table, right in the middle, where it cannot be overlooked, moving the vase of roses a little way back. As for her own goodbye letter, written on such a shabby little Post-it Note that her children will spend a long time looking for another, real letter, she puts it on the table beside my grandfather's.

‡

At 7.35 my grandmother closes the bedroom door behind her. All the lights are on, the two lamps on the bedside table, the standard lamp beside the desk, the big round ceiling lamp. She sits down on the bed again. Two glasses full of water, with a layer of white powder at the bottom of each glass, still stand on her bedside table. She takes the spoon lying ready and stirs first one glass, then the other, until the powder has dispersed in the water.

My grandfather is watching from his side of the bed, the left-hand side. He has pulled the covers well up to his throat so that only his head is showing.

'You'll have to drink fast.' With these words she hands him one glass and takes the other herself.

'Just a moment.' She slips her legs under the covers. Now they are lying side by side in bed, each holding a glass.

She can feel the sleeping tablets working now, their effect beginning to spread inside her head.

'Pista?'

He hears her as is if through a mist.

'Yes?'

'Now,' she says.

They both raise their glasses to their mouths and drink the contents straight down, as it says in the book. They were prepared for the bitter taste, and it's not as bad as all that. They put the glasses down on their bedside tables.

'Pista?'

Her hand reaches for his.

'Yes?'

It is quieter inside her head now. All the lights are on, but it seems to her that it has just become a little darker.

'Pista?'

She takes his hand.

He would like to look at her, but he is so tired all of a sudden. So tired.

'Thank you.'

He feels her pressing his hand.

'No,' he says. 'I thank you.'

Darkness falls.

She closes her eyes.

‡

On 14 October 1991, a Monday, the newspaper boy threw the *Berlingske Tidende* over the garden fence as he did early every weekday morning. He aimed at the front door as well as he could, but today his aim was not quite accurate, and the newspaper landed a good two metres away, on the stone steps leading up to the house.

‡

On Tuesday 15 October 1991 the same newspaper boy took rather better aim, and the newspaper landed right in the middle of the doormat. Now there were two newspapers lying outside Number 82, since the day before's newspaper had not been taken in, and it was still lying on the steps in front of the door.

‡

On the afternoon of the same day, Tuesday 15 October 1991, the telephone in my grandparents' house rang at about five o'clock.

That was me.

I was sitting on the green corduroy sofa in Munich, which still stands in my parents' home in front of the desk with the telephone on it, and I had the brown leather-bound telephone book of numbers open in front of me at A. I had just had a call from my cousin in Denmark. He wanted to know if by any chance our grandparents were with us in Munich. He hadn't been able to get hold of them, and he and his father had just driven out to their house, but no one opened the door, and so he had wondered if they might perhaps be with us.

No, they weren't here, I had said as normally as possible. We both acted as if we didn't know what that meant, and we hung up quickly.

Then I had looked up my grandparents' number in my parents' brown leather telephone book. I didn't know it by heart because back then long-distance calls were something special, and we didn't often call each other.

I dialled.

Their telephone rang.

I knew that no one would pick it up.

It rang for a long time; my grandparents didn't have an answering machine. I imagined the phone ringing in their house where it stood on the desk in their living room, ringing loud and long, a ring-tone that could be heard clearly in every last corner of every room.

In the kitchen, where the toaster had been disconnected.

In the guestroom, where the Chagall print hung.

In the hall, where the skull lay on its shelf.

In the guest toilet with its blue tiles.

In the bathroom, where a large bottle of 'Nur 1 Tropfen' mouthwash stood beside the toothbrush glass.

In the dining room, where the sheet music of the Diabelli Variations lay on top of the piano.

In their bedroom.

I sat in Munich on the green corduroy sofa in my parents' living room, with the receiver to my ear, the telephone rang in Copenhagen, and I dared not hang up.

FROM THE POLICE FILES

Directly after the telephone call on Tuesday 15.10.91, at 17.27 hours, Superintendent Søren J. and the undersigned, in Car No. 305, and Carsten A. in Car No. 305, were sent to the notified address in Charlottenlund by Superintendent T. who was on duty at the police station. We arrived at around 17.40 hours.

Outside the house we met the man who had made the call, Peter D., resident in Hellerup, and his son, the grand-child of the (deceased) couple, Sebastian D., resident in Brabrand.

They made a statement to our colleague Superintendent Søren J.

Superintendent Søren J. and the undersigned, as well as duty officer Superintendent Carsten A., walked all round the house to see if we could get in or see anything through the windows. There were lights on almost all over the house, the curtains were all drawn except in the living room, which looked neat and tidy, there was no one to be seen in the living room. It was not possible to see through the windows of the rooms because, as mentioned above, the curtains were drawn.

The front door was locked, and so were several doors to the terrace and garden. Outside the front door there were two damp newspapers, the *Berlingske Tidende* of 14.10.91 and 15.10.91.

Duty officer Superintendent Carsten A. had a locksmith called in.

Locksmith M. arrived at 18.00 hours. The door was open soon afterwards, and duty officer Superintendent Carsten A. then went into the house alone and found the two deceased dead in bed.

Duty officer Carsten A. had previously said he would go into the house alone, because there was a chance that this might be a case of a different kind.

Superintendent Søren J. and the undersigned then entered the room where duty officer Superintendent Carsten A. showed us the deceased lying in the bedroom. Superintendent Søren J. then returned to the caller and the grandson.

The caller and the grandson then went into the bedroom, where they identified the deceased. A note was found on the bedroom door with the following wording:

'Please do not try to revive us,' dated 13.10.91, and signed.

The said note was identified as written by the (deceased) woman, the signature could not be deciphered but was recognised by the caller and the grandson.

The said note was added to the case file.

Death was established by duty officer Carsten A. at 18.04 hours. I and duty officer Carsten A. established the signs of death, there was livor mortis on the lower parts of the bodies, advanced rigor mortis was present, they were both cold. Discolouration / livor mortis on the left hand of the lady, hanging down. When the quilt was taken off the lady, black toes were visible. When the quilt had been removed, discolouration of the feet suddenly increased. It was also cold in the bedroom. Both had livor mortis marks down in the stomach area.

On the grounds of the above observations, duty officer Superintendent Carsten A. had a mortuary van summoned.

The two deceased, as mentioned above, were found lying in bed in the bedroom.

They were both lying under the quilt with only their heads showing. They were holding each other by the hand.

The man was lying on his back, wearing striped pyjamas, and holding his wife's hand with his left hand.

The woman was lying on her right side, holding her right hand and arm up to her head. Her left arm was outstretched, and she was holding her husband's hand with her left hand. The woman wore a pale nightdress.

On the woman's bedside table in the bedroom, various medicines were found, as well as a syringe in a beaker. The pills as well as the above-mentioned syringe were brought back here. The syringe was empty, with a protective case round the canula. Both the deceased had a half-full glass of water on their bedside tables, both also had a smaller glass in which it could be seen that pills or other substances had been crushed with a spoon or pulverised. Remains of a white substance were visible in these glasses, and they and the spoon were brought here.

An oxygen inhaler was found near the bed on the dead man's side.

The house is a single-storey building, situated in a leafy district of villas.

The house lay a little way back from the street, on a slight rise.

The house is a wooden house painted brown.

It was possible to walk all the way round the house, which is built in a horseshoe shape.

All the windows in the house were closed and fastened with hooks inside. They were all intact.

A search of the house and investigation of means of access to it produced nothing to suggest that anyone had broken in.

It was very attractive and tidy, there was no indication that acts of violence, etc., had taken place.

The deceased couple's dog was not found in or near the house. The house has a garage on the street. The deceased's car was parked in the garage. The garage door was locked.

It should be noted that in one room various presents for family and friends of the deceased were arranged on a table.

A sketch of the house is appended to this report.

‡

The last sheet of paper in the file drawn up by the Danish police on my grandparents' suicide, now in the archives in Helsingör, is the bill sent by the locksmith who opened the door. It cost 297.02 kroner.

Acknowledgements

My thanks to Lily Brett for the inspiration, to my father for his courage, my mother for her support, Zsuzsi for her patience and hospitality, to all who have taken the time to tell me about my grandparents, Stephen-István for all the information, Petra Eggers for her company, Georg Reuchlein for his confidence, Martin Mittelmeier for his clever comments, Charlotte for reading the book at an early stage, and Olivier, just because.

About the Translator

Anthea Bell (OBE) is an award-winning translator whose translations incude Sebald's *Austerlitz*, Cornelia Funke's *Inkworld* trilogy and the *Asterix* comics.